IMPORTANT NOTICE / DISCLAIMER

This book is provided for informational and educational purposes only.

It is not medical advice, psychological advice, psychiatric advice, legal advice, or financial advice. It is not a substitute for professional care.

If you are experiencing severe distress, thoughts of self-harm, or are in crisis, seek immediate help from emergency services or qualified professionals.

Results vary by individual. The system is designed as a structured reference tool. Use it responsibly and conservatively, especially when you are under high stress or emotionally unstable.

By using this book, you accept full responsibility for your choices and outcomes.

Author: James Hutchinson

Series: The Advanced Grabovoi Codes Reference (CRP Structural Codes™ System)

DEDICATION

For the people rebuilding themselves quietly. For the ones learning stability the hard way.

HOW THIS VOLUME IS BUILT

Volume III is designed like a manual.

You are not meant to "read it through."
You are meant to:

1) Identify a subsystem (what you're working on)

2) Select a function (what you want to do)

3) Select an intensity (how hard to push)

4) Apply with controlled stacking

5) Track stability, then adjust

This volume prioritizes:

Emotional stability first.

Identity coherence second.

Acceleration only after baseline control.

THE CRP STRUCTURAL CODES™ FORMAT (DDSSFI VVV + CHECK DIGIT)

Every entry uses a 9-digit structural code:

D SS F I VVV C

D = Domain (1 digit)

SS = Subsystem (2 digits)

F = Function (1 digit)

I = Intensity (1 digit)

VVV = Variant (3 digits)

C = Check Digit (Option B)

Volume III uses:

Domain 02 (Emotional & Identity) → D = 2

Check Digit:

Option B (VC-20 cycle keyed to Variant VVV)

FUNCTION TYPES (F)

1 — Stabilize

2 — Increase

3 — Decrease

4 — Repair

5 — Protect

6 — Amplify

7 — Recalibrate

8 — Accelerate

INTENSITY CLASSES (I)

Class I (1) — Gentle Calibration

Class II (2) — Standard Structural Activation

Class III (3) — High-Intensity Structural Shift

Rule:

Class III is limited and must be buffered by Class I/II.

QUICK START (60 SECONDS)

If you are emotionally unstable right now:

1) Choose a "reduction" entry:

Function 3 (Decrease) — Class I or II

2) Add a baseline anchor:

Function 1 (Stabilize) — Class I or II

3) Optional containment:

Function 5 (Protect) — Class II

Max 2–3 sequences total.

Max 1 Class III at a time.

STACKING RULES (NON-NEGOTIABLE)

Maximum concurrent sequences: 3

Maximum Class III sequences at once: 1

If you feel worse (wired, agitated, insomnia, panic):

Drop Accelerate first, then drop Class III.

Crash reset protocol (48 hours):

Decrease → Stabilize → Protect

HOW TO USE THIS AS A REFERENCE

Use the Table of Contents to find the subsystem.

Use the Functional Index when you know the function type.

Use the Intensity Index when you need stability control.

Use the Thematic Keyword Index when you only know the symptom pattern.

Use the Numerical Code Index for exact retrieval.

TABLE OF CONTENTS — VOLUME III

Emotional & Identity Calibration (Domain 02)

PART I — CODED SUBSYSTEMS (DOMAIN 02)

PART II — INDEX ARCHITECTURE

APPENDICES (SYSTEM-WIDE)

Appendix F — Scaling Framework (Summary)

Back Matter

Final System Note

Series Roadmap

About the Author

Review Request

SERIES ROADMAP (SHORT)

Volume I — Financial Optimization

Volume II — Biological & Nervous System

Volume III — Emotional & Identity Calibration

Volume IV — Cognitive & Strategic Performance

Volume V — Advanced Structural Calibration

ABOUT THE AUTHOR

James Hutchinson builds structured reference systems.

This series is designed to be indexed, classified, and usable under real-world pressure.

02-01 Emotional Baseline Stabilization

Domain 02 — Emotional & Identity

Focus:
• baseline steadiness
• volatility reduction
• rebound speed after stress
• containment first
• escalation prevention

Entry 1

Structural Code: **201120014**
Catalog ID: **CRP-02-01-0001**
Function: Stabilize (1)
Intensity: Class II
Variant: 001

Emotional Baseline Stability Anchor

Supports a steadier emotional baseline through the day.

Entry 2

Structural Code: **201220027**
Catalog ID: **CRP-02-01-0002**
Function: Increase (2)
Intensity: Class II
Variant: 002

Emotional Stability Capacity Increase

Increases tolerance for emotional load without destabilizing.

Entry 3

Structural Code: **201310035**
Catalog ID: **CRP-02-01-0003**
Function: Decrease (3)
Intensity: Class I
Variant: 003

Volatility Reduction

Reduces spike-and-crash emotional swing patterns.

Entry 4

Structural Code: **201420046**
Catalog ID: **CRP-02-01-0004**
Function: Repair (4)
Intensity: Class II
Variant: 004

Baseline Recovery Reset

Supports return to baseline after disruption.

Entry 5

Structural Code: **201520053**
Catalog ID: **CRP-02-01-0005**
Function: Protect (5)
Intensity: Class II
Variant: 005

Emotional Containment Shield

Protects baseline steadiness during pressure events.

Entry 6

Structural Code: **201620069**
Catalog ID: **CRP-02-01-0006**
Function: Amplify (6)
Intensity: Class II
Variant: 006

Calm Signal Amplifier

Strengthens access to calm-state consistency.

Entry 7

Structural Code: **201710076**
Catalog ID: **CRP-02-01-0007**
Function: Recalibrate (7)
Intensity: Class I
Variant: 007

Baseline Set-Point Calibration

Aligns emotional set-point toward steadier default.

Entry 8

Structural Code: **201810088**
Catalog ID: **CRP-02-01-0008**
Function: Accelerate (8)
Intensity: Class I
Variant: 008

Downshift Acceleration (Emotional)

Improves speed of calming after activation.

Entry 9

Structural Code: **201230094**
Catalog ID: **CRP-02-01-0009**
Function: Increase (2)

Intensity: Class III
Variant: 009

High-Stability Surge

High-intensity reinforcement of stable emotional baseline.

Entry 10

Structural Code: **201320103**
Catalog ID: **CRP-02-01-0010**
Function: Decrease (3)
Intensity: Class II
Variant: 010

Reactivity Reduction

Reduces fast-trigger reactivity and escalation.

Entry 11

Structural Code: **201530114**
Catalog ID: **CRP-02-01-0011**
Function: Protect (5)
Intensity: Class III
Variant: 011

Baseline Integrity Lock

Deep protection of emotional baseline under stress.

Entry 12

Structural Code: **201620127**
Catalog ID: **CRP-02-01-0012**
Function: Amplify (6)
Intensity: Class II
Variant: 012

Regulation Efficiency Amplifier

Strengthens the ability to regulate without suppression.

Entry 13

Structural Code: **201410136**
Catalog ID: **CRP-02-01-0013**
Function: Repair (4)
Intensity: Class I
Variant: 013

Aftershock Recovery Reset

Supports recovery after emotional aftereffects.

Entry 14

Structural Code: **201720145**
Catalog ID: **CRP-02-01-0014**
Function: Recalibrate (7)

Intensity: Class II
Variant: 014

Emotional Range Calibration

Aligns range toward stability without flattening.

Entry 15

Structural Code: **201110154**
Catalog ID: **CRP-02-01-0015**
Function: Stabilize (1)
Intensity: Class I
Variant: 015

Daily Baseline Anchor

Reinforces a stable emotional default each day.

Entry 16

Structural Code: **201820163**
Catalog ID: **CRP-02-01-0016**
Function: Accelerate (8)
Intensity: Class II
Variant: 016

Recovery Speed Boost (Emotional)

Improves rebound speed after stress spikes.

Entry 17

Structural Code: **201220172**
Catalog ID: **CRP-02-01-0017**
Function: Increase (2)
Intensity: Class II
Variant: 017

Composure Capacity Increase

Increases ability to hold composure under pressure.

Entry 18

Structural Code: **201320181**
Catalog ID: **CRP-02-01-0018**
Function: Decrease (3)
Intensity: Class II
Variant: 018

Emotional Noise Reduction

Reduces background emotional interference and instability.

Entry 19

Structural Code: **201610196**
Catalog ID: **CRP-02-01-0019**
Function: Amplify (6)
Intensity: Class I
Variant: 019

Calm Discipline Reinforcement

Strengthens consistent calm maintenance habits.

Entry 20

Structural Code: **201530205**
Catalog ID: **CRP-02-01-0020**
Function: Protect (5)
Intensity: Class III
Variant: 020

Emotional Sovereignty Anchor

Deep reinforcement of long-term emotional baseline stability.

02-02 Anxiety Loop Reduction

Domain 02 — Emotional & Identity

Focus:
- rumination interruption
- threat-signal downshift
- panic loop control
- body-mind escalation reduction
- return-to-baseline speed

Entry 1

Structural Code: **202120014**
Catalog ID: **CRP-02-02-0001**
Function: Stabilize (1)
Intensity: Class II
Variant: 001

Anxiety Baseline Stability Anchor

Stabilizes baseline anxiety levels across the day.

Entry 2

Structural Code: **202220027**
Catalog ID: **CRP-02-02-0002**
Function: Increase (2)

Intensity: Class II
Variant: 002

Calm Tolerance Capacity Increase

Increases tolerance for uncertainty without escalation.

Entry 3

Structural Code: **202310035**
Catalog ID: **CRP-02-02-0003**
Function: Decrease (3)
Intensity: Class I
Variant: 003

Rumination Reduction

Reduces repetitive looping thoughts and mental replay.

Entry 4

Structural Code: **202420046**
Catalog ID: **CRP-02-02-0004**
Function: Repair (4)
Intensity: Class II
Variant: 004

Loop Interruption Recovery Reset

Supports reset after an anxiety spiral episode.

Entry 5

Structural Code: **202520053**
Catalog ID: **CRP-02-02-0005**
Function: Protect (5)
Intensity: Class II
Variant: 005

Anxiety Containment Shield

Protects stability during triggering conditions.

Entry 6

Structural Code: **202620069**
Catalog ID: **CRP-02-02-0006**
Function: Amplify (6)
Intensity: Class II
Variant: 006

Regulation Signal Amplifier

Strengthens ability to regulate without force.

Entry 7

Structural Code: **202710076**
Catalog ID: **CRP-02-02-0007**
Function: Recalibrate (7)
Intensity: Class I
Variant: 007

Threat Appraisal Calibration

Aligns threat perception toward realistic signal.

Entry 8

Structural Code: **202810088**
Catalog ID: **CRP-02-02-0008**
Function: Accelerate (8)
Intensity: Class I
Variant: 008

Downshift Acceleration (Anxiety)

Improves speed of calming after activation.

Entry 9

Structural Code: **202230094**
Catalog ID: **CRP-02-02-0009**
Function: Increase (2)
Intensity: Class III
Variant: 009

High-Stability Calm Surge

High-intensity reinforcement of calm access under pressure.

Entry 10

Structural Code: **202320103**
Catalog ID: **CRP-02-02-0010**
Function: Decrease (3)
Intensity: Class II
Variant: 010

Panic Reactivity Reduction

Reduces body-mind escalation and adrenaline spikes.

Entry 11

Structural Code: **202530114**
Catalog ID: **CRP-02-02-0011**
Function: Protect (5)
Intensity: Class III
Variant: 011

Loop Lockout Shield

Deep protection against repeated spiral cycling.

Entry 12

Structural Code: **202620127**
Catalog ID: **CRP-02-02-0012**
Function: Amplify (6)
Intensity: Class II
Variant: 012

Cognitive Quiet Amplifier

Strengthens mental quiet and reduces intrusive noise.

Entry 13

Structural Code: **202410136**
Catalog ID: **CRP-02-02-0013**
Function: Repair (4)
Intensity: Class I
Variant: 013

After-Spike Recovery Reset

Supports stabilization after panic symptoms subside.

Entry 14

Structural Code: **202720145**
Catalog ID: **CRP-02-02-0014**
Function: Recalibrate (7)
Intensity: Class II
Variant: 014

Uncertainty Tolerance Calibration

Aligns response away from catastrophizing.

Entry 15

Structural Code: **202110154**
Catalog ID: **CRP-02-02-0015**
Function: Stabilize (1)
Intensity: Class I
Variant: 015

Daily Calm Anchor

Reinforces a steadier calm baseline each day.

Entry 16

Structural Code: **202820163**
Catalog ID: **CRP-02-02-0016**
Function: Accelerate (8)

Intensity: Class II
Variant: 016

Spiral Exit Speed Boost

Improves speed of exiting anxiety loops.

Entry 17

Structural Code: **202220172**
Catalog ID: **CRP-02-02-0017**
Function: Increase (2)
Intensity: Class II
Variant: 017

Nervous Tolerance Increase

Increases capacity to hold steady during stress signals.

Entry 18

Structural Code: **202320181**
Catalog ID: **CRP-02-02-0018**
Function: Decrease (3)
Intensity: Class II
Variant: 018

Intrusive Thought Reduction

Reduces involuntary threat-thought intrusion patterns.

Entry 19

Structural Code: **202610196**
Catalog ID: **CRP-02-02-0019**
Function: Amplify (6)
Intensity: Class I
Variant: 019

Regulation Discipline Reinforcement

Strengthens consistent regulation behavior under pressure.

Entry 20

Structural Code: **202530205**
Catalog ID: **CRP-02-02-0020**
Function: Protect (5)
Intensity: Class III
Variant: 020

Anxiety Sovereignty Anchor

Deep reinforcement of long-term loop control and calm baseline.

02-03 Trauma Load Containment

Domain 02 — Emotional & Identity

Focus:
- containment without suppression
- reducing flashback intensity
- nervous system safety restoration
- emotional aftershock recovery
- controlled processing (no flooding)

Entry 1

Structural Code: **203120014**
Catalog ID: **CRP-02-03-0001**
Function: Stabilize (1)
Intensity: Class II
Variant: 001

Trauma Load Stabilization Anchor

Stabilizes emotional load and reduces internal volatility.

Entry 2

Structural Code: **203220027**
Catalog ID: **CRP-02-03-0002**

Function: Increase (2)
Intensity: Class II
Variant: 002

Containment Capacity Increase

Increases capacity to hold intensity without flooding.

Entry 3

Structural Code: **203310035**
Catalog ID: **CRP-02-03-0003**
Function: Decrease (3)
Intensity: Class I
Variant: 003

Flashback Intensity Reduction

Reduces severity of intrusive memory activation.

Entry 4

Structural Code: **203420046**
Catalog ID: **CRP-02-03-0004**
Function: Repair (4)
Intensity: Class II
Variant: 004

Aftershock Recovery Reset

Supports stabilization after a trigger episode.

Entry 5

Structural Code: **203520053**
Catalog ID: **CRP-02-03-0005**
Function: Protect (5)
Intensity: Class II
Variant: 005

Containment Shield

Protects nervous system stability during exposure windows.

Entry 6

Structural Code: **203620069**
Catalog ID: **CRP-02-03-0006**
Function: Amplify (6)
Intensity: Class II
Variant: 006

Safety Signal Amplifier

Strengthens internal safety perception and steadiness.

Entry 7

Structural Code: **203710076**
Catalog ID: **CRP-02-03-0007**
Function: Recalibrate (7)
Intensity: Class I
Variant: 007

Threat Memory Calibration

Aligns memory-trigger response toward present safety.

Entry 8

Structural Code: **203810088**
Catalog ID: **CRP-02-03-0008**
Function: Accelerate (8)
Intensity: Class I
Variant: 008

Downshift Acceleration (Trauma)

Improves speed of calming after trigger activation.

Entry 9

Structural Code: **203230094**
Catalog ID: **CRP-02-03-0009**
Function: Increase (2)
Intensity: Class III
Variant: 009

High-Containment Surge

High-intensity reinforcement of containment capacity.

Entry 10

Structural Code: **203320103**
Catalog ID: **CRP-02-03-0010**
Function: Decrease (3)
Intensity: Class II
Variant: 010

Hypervigilance Reduction

Reduces scanning, tension, and threat anticipation.

Entry 11

Structural Code: **203530114**
Catalog ID: **CRP-02-03-0011**
Function: Protect (5)
Intensity: Class III
Variant: 011

Trauma Loop Lockout Shield

Deep protection against repeated re-trigger cycling.

Entry 12

Structural Code: **203620127**
Catalog ID: **CRP-02-03-0012**
Function: Amplify (6)
Intensity: Class II
Variant: 012

Grounding Signal Amplifier

Strengthens present-moment anchoring and body safety.

Entry 13

Structural Code: **203410136**
Catalog ID: **CRP-02-03-0013**
Function: Repair (4)
Intensity: Class I
Variant: 013

Trigger Residue Repair

Supports recovery from lingering emotional residue.

Entry 14

Structural Code: **203720145**
Catalog ID: **CRP-02-03-0014**
Function: Recalibrate (7)
Intensity: Class II
Variant: 014

Safety Baseline Calibration

Aligns internal safety set-point toward stability.

Entry 15

Structural Code: **203110154**
Catalog ID: **CRP-02-03-0015**
Function: Stabilize (1)
Intensity: Class I
Variant: 015

Daily Containment Anchor

Reinforces steady containment as a daily baseline.

Entry 16

Structural Code: **203820163**
Catalog ID: **CRP-02-03-0016**
Function: Accelerate (8)
Intensity: Class II
Variant: 016

Recovery Speed Boost (Trauma)

Improves recovery speed after activation events.

Entry 17

Structural Code: **203220172**
Catalog ID: **CRP-02-03-0017**
Function: Increase (2)
Intensity: Class II
Variant: 017

Emotional Load Tolerance Increase

Increases tolerance for difficult emotions without collapse.

Entry 18

Structural Code: **203320181**
Catalog ID: **CRP-02-03-0018**
Function: Decrease (3)
Intensity: Class II
Variant: 018

Intrusion Frequency Reduction

Reduces frequency of unwanted intrusive recall.

Entry 19

Structural Code: **203610196**
Catalog ID: **CRP-02-03-0019**
Function: Amplify (6)

Intensity: Class I
Variant: 019

Safety Discipline Reinforcement

Strengthens consistent practices that maintain internal safety.

Entry 20

Structural Code: **203530205**
Catalog ID: **CRP-02-03-0020**
Function: Protect (5)
Intensity: Class III
Variant: 020

Trauma Sovereignty Anchor

Deep reinforcement of long-term containment and stability.

02-04 Confidence & Authority Calibration

Domain 02 — Emotional & Identity

Focus:
• confidence baseline stabilization
• authority signal strengthening
• shame interference reduction
• social pressure resilience
• decisive action support

Entry 1

Structural Code: **204120014**
Catalog ID: **CRP-02-04-0001**
Function: Stabilize (1)
Intensity: Class II
Variant: 001

Confidence Baseline Anchor

Stabilizes confidence as a daily default state.

Entry 2

Structural Code: **204220027**
Catalog ID: **CRP-02-04-0002**
Function: Increase (2)

Intensity: Class II
Variant: 002

Authority Signal Increase

Increases presence, clarity, and self-trust under observation.

Entry 3

Structural Code: **204310035**
Catalog ID: **CRP-02-04-0003**
Function: Decrease (3)
Intensity: Class I
Variant: 003

Self-Doubt Reduction

Reduces internal doubt loops and second-guessing.

Entry 4

Structural Code: **204420046**
Catalog ID: **CRP-02-04-0004**
Function: Repair (4)
Intensity: Class II
Variant: 004

Confidence Recovery Reset

Supports recovery after embarrassment, rejection, or perceived failure.

Entry 5

Structural Code: **204520053**
Catalog ID: **CRP-02-04-0005**
Function: Protect (5)
Intensity: Class II
Variant: 005

Authority Containment Shield

Protects composure during confrontation and high scrutiny.

Entry 6

Structural Code: **204620069**
Catalog ID: **CRP-02-04-0006**
Function: Amplify (6)
Intensity: Class II
Variant: 006

Presence Amplifier

Strengthens calm presence and command signal without aggression.

Entry 7

Structural Code: **204710076**
Catalog ID: **CRP-02-04-0007**
Function: Recalibrate (7)
Intensity: Class I
Variant: 007

Status Perception Calibration

Recalibrates perceived hierarchy pressure and reduces intimidation response.

Entry 8

Structural Code: **204810088**
Catalog ID: **CRP-02-04-0008**
Function: Accelerate (8)
Intensity: Class I
Variant: 008

Confidence Onset Acceleration

Improves speed of shifting into a confident state when needed.

Entry 9

Structural Code: **204230094**
Catalog ID: **CRP-02-04-0009**
Function: Increase (2)
Intensity: Class III
Variant: 009

High-Authority Surge

High-intensity reinforcement of authority signal and decisiveness.

Entry 10

Structural Code: **204320103**
Catalog ID: **CRP-02-04-0010**
Function: Decrease (3)
Intensity: Class II
Variant: 010

Social Threat Reactivity Reduction

Reduces fear response to judgment, conflict, or evaluation.

Entry 11

Structural Code: **204530114**
Catalog ID: **CRP-02-04-0011**
Function: Protect (5)
Intensity: Class III
Variant: 011

Authority Integrity Lock

Deep protection against collapse under pressure or criticism.

Entry 12

Structural Code: **204620127**
Catalog ID: **CRP-02-04-0012**
Function: Amplify (6)
Intensity: Class II
Variant: 012

Command Clarity Amplifier

Strengthens clarity of speech, posture, and internal certainty.

Entry 13

Structural Code: **204410136**
Catalog ID: **CRP-02-04-0013**
Function: Repair (4)
Intensity: Class I
Variant: 013

Shame Residue Repair

Repairs lingering shame after social exposure or mistakes.

Entry 14

Structural Code: **204720145**
Catalog ID: **CRP-02-04-0014**
Function: Recalibrate (7)

Intensity: Class II
Variant: 014

Assertiveness Calibration

Aligns response toward clean boundaries without overcorrection.

Entry 15

Structural Code: **204110154**
Catalog ID: **CRP-02-04-0015**
Function: Stabilize (1)
Intensity: Class I
Variant: 015

Daily Authority Anchor

Reinforces authority as a stable daily baseline.

Entry 16

Structural Code: **204820163**
Catalog ID: **CRP-02-04-0016**
Function: Accelerate (8)
Intensity: Class II
Variant: 016

Decisive Action Boost

Improves speed of decision and execution under social pressure.

Entry 17

Structural Code: **204220172**
Catalog ID: **CRP-02-04-0017**
Function: Increase (2)
Intensity: Class II
Variant: 017

Self-Trust Capacity Increase

Increases trust in judgment and reduces permission-seeking.

Entry 18

Structural Code: **204320181**
Catalog ID: **CRP-02-04-0018**
Function: Decrease (3)
Intensity: Class II
Variant: 018

People-Pleasing Reduction

Reduces compliance drift and improves boundary stability.

Entry 19

Structural Code: **204610196**
Catalog ID: **CRP-02-04-0019**
Function: Amplify (6)

Intensity: Class I
Variant: 019

Confidence Discipline Reinforcement

Strengthens consistent confident behavior patterns over time.

Entry 20

Structural Code: **204530205**
Catalog ID: **CRP-02-04-0020**
Function: Protect (5)
Intensity: Class III
Variant: 020

Sovereign Authority Anchor

Deep reinforcement of long-term authority stability and self-command.

02-05 Scarcity Imprint Deconstruction

Domain 02 — Emotional & Identity

Focus:
• scarcity reflex interruption
• threat-money coupling reduction
• income safety pattern repair
• abundance identity stabilization
• decision-making under resource pressure

Entry 1

Structural Code: **205120014**
Catalog ID: **CRP-02-05-0001**
Function: Stabilize (1)
Intensity: Class II
Variant: 001

Scarcity Reflex Stabilization Anchor

Stabilizes the automatic scarcity response when money pressure appears.

Entry 2

Structural Code: **205220027**
Catalog ID: **CRP-02-05-0002**
Function: Increase (2)
Intensity: Class II
Variant: 002

Abundance Tolerance Capacity Increase

Increases tolerance for receiving, holding, and expanding resources without collapse.

Entry 3

Structural Code: **205310035**
Catalog ID: **CRP-02-05-0003**
Function: Decrease (3)
Intensity: Class I
Variant: 003

Panic-Spend Impulse Reduction

Reduces urgency-driven spending, reactive purchases, and "escape buying."

Entry 4

Structural Code: **205420046**
Catalog ID: **CRP-02-05-0004**
Function: Repair (4)

Intensity: Class II
Variant: 004

Scarcity Pattern Repair Reset

Repairs residue from long scarcity periods and resets baseline expectation.

Entry 5

Structural Code: **205520053**
Catalog ID: **CRP-02-05-0005**
Function: Protect (5)
Intensity: Class II
Variant: 005

Resource Safety Containment Shield

Protects stability during bills, debt pressure, and uncertain income periods.

Entry 6

Structural Code: **205620069**
Catalog ID: **CRP-02-05-0006**
Function: Amplify (6)
Intensity: Class II
Variant: 006

Security Signal Amplifier

Strengthens internal safety signal so money decisions become cleaner and less emotional.

Entry 7

Structural Code: **205710076**
Catalog ID: **CRP-02-05-0007**
Function: Recalibrate (7)
Intensity: Class I
Variant: 007

Worth-Resource Calibration

Recalibrates self-worth linkage to money so identity stops fluctuating with cashflow.

Entry 8

Structural Code: **205810088**
Catalog ID: **CRP-02-05-0008**
Function: Accelerate (8)
Intensity: Class I
Variant: 008

Calm Finance Response Acceleration

Accelerates the shift from threat-response to regulated decision mode.

Entry 9

Structural Code: **205230094**
Catalog ID: **CRP-02-05-0009**
Function: Increase (2)
Intensity: Class III
Variant: 009

High-Capacity Receiving Surge

High-intensity increase of "receiving bandwidth" without sabotage reflex.

Entry 10

Structural Code: **205320103**
Catalog ID: **CRP-02-05-0010**
Function: Decrease (3)
Intensity: Class II
Variant: 010

Scarcity Rumination Reduction

Reduces obsessive counting, worry loops, and "future catastrophe" forecasting.

Entry 11

Structural Code: **205530114**
Catalog ID: **CRP-02-05-0011**
Function: Protect (5)
Intensity: Class III
Variant: 011

Scarcity Loop Lockout Shield

Deep protection against repeated relapse into scarcity identity during stress.

Entry 12

Structural Code: **205620127**
Catalog ID: **CRP-02-05-0012**
Function: Amplify (6)
Intensity: Class II
Variant: 012

Long-Horizon Thinking Amplifier

Amplifies long-range planning signal over short-term panic reactions.

Entry 13

Structural Code: **205410136**
Catalog ID: **CRP-02-05-0013**
Function: Repair (4)
Intensity: Class I
Variant: 013

Debt-Shame Residue Repair

Repairs shame residue tied to debt, mistakes, or past financial instability.

Entry 14

Structural Code: **205720145**
Catalog ID: **CRP-02-05-0014**
Function: Recalibrate (7)
Intensity: Class II
Variant: 014

Money Threat Recalibration

Recalibrates money signals away from danger framing and into neutral operational framing.

Entry 15

Structural Code: **205110154**
Catalog ID: **CRP-02-05-0015**
Function: Stabilize (1)
Intensity: Class I
Variant: 015

Daily Abundance Baseline Anchor

Reinforces a stable "enoughness" baseline as a daily default.

Entry 16

Structural Code: **205820163**
Catalog ID: **CRP-02-05-0016**
Function: Accelerate (8)
Intensity: Class II
Variant: 016

Scarcity Exit Speed Boost

Improves speed of exiting scarcity states after triggers (bills, late notices, income dips).

Entry 17

Structural Code: **205220172**
Catalog ID: **CRP-02-05-0017**
Function: Increase (2)
Intensity: Class II
Variant: 017

Resource Stability Capacity Increase

Increases ability to hold steady as income grows (prevents "bigger money, bigger panic").

Entry 18

Structural Code: **205320181**
Catalog ID: **CRP-02-05-0018**
Function: Decrease (3)
Intensity: Class II
Variant: 018

Self-Sabotage Spend Reduction

Reduces sabotage patterns: splurging after wins, undoing progress, "back to zero" cycles.

Entry 19

Structural Code: **205610196**
Catalog ID: **CRP-02-05-0019**
Function: Amplify (6)
Intensity: Class I
Variant: 019

Financial Discipline Signal Reinforcement

Strengthens steady execution: budgeting, tracking, follow-through, and delayed gratification.

Entry 20

Structural Code: **205530205**
Catalog ID: **CRP-02-05-0020**
Function: Protect (5)
Intensity: Class III
Variant: 020

Abundance Identity Lock

Deep reinforcement of a stable abundance identity under pressure and volatility.

02-06 Identity Stability Reinforcement

Domain 02 — Emotional & Identity

Focus:
- identity coherence under pressure
- reducing self-contradiction and drift
- stabilizing standards + boundaries
- strengthening follow-through signal
- preventing regression after wins

Entry 1

Structural Code: **206120014**
Catalog ID: **CRP-02-06-0001**
Function: Stabilize (1)
Intensity: Class II
Variant: 001

Identity Coherence Anchor

Stabilizes identity signal so decisions stay consistent across moods and stress.

Entry 2

Structural Code: **206220027**
Catalog ID: **CRP-02-06-0002**
Function: Increase (2)

Intensity: Class II
Variant: 002

Identity Strength Capacity Increase

Increases capacity to hold a stable self-definition without collapse or drift.

Entry 3

Structural Code: **206310035**
Catalog ID: **CRP-02-06-0003**
Function: Decrease (3)
Intensity: Class I
Variant: 003

Identity Drift Reduction

Reduces "different person every day" variability and unstable self-story shifts.

Entry 4

Structural Code: **206420046**
Catalog ID: **CRP-02-06-0004**
Function: Repair (4)
Intensity: Class II
Variant: 004

Self-Concept Repair Reset

Repairs identity fragmentation after stress, failure, or prolonged instability.

Entry 5

Structural Code: **206520053**
Catalog ID: **CRP-02-06-0005**
Function: Protect (5)
Intensity: Class II
Variant: 005

Identity Boundary Shield

Protects identity stability from external pressure, persuasion, and social distortion.

Entry 6

Structural Code: **206620069**
Catalog ID: **CRP-02-06-0006**
Function: Amplify (6)
Intensity: Class II
Variant: 006

Consistency Signal Amplifier

Strengthens consistency of behavior so identity becomes observable and reliable.

Entry 7

Structural Code: **206710076**
Catalog ID: **CRP-02-06-0007**
Function: Recalibrate (7)
Intensity: Class I
Variant: 007

Standards Calibration

Recalibrates standards upward without perfectionism or collapse cycles.

Entry 8

Structural Code: **206810088**
Catalog ID: **CRP-02-06-0008**
Function: Accelerate (8)
Intensity: Class I
Variant: 008

Identity Re-Alignment Acceleration

Accelerates return to "who you are" after distraction, drift, or disruption.

Entry 9

Structural Code: **206230094**
Catalog ID: **CRP-02-06-0009**
Function: Increase (2)
Intensity: Class III
Variant: 009

High-Coherence Surge

High-intensity reinforcement of identity clarity, commitment, and follow-through.

Entry 10

Structural Code: **206320103**
Catalog ID: **CRP-02-06-0010**
Function: Decrease (3)
Intensity: Class II
Variant: 010

Self-Contradiction Reduction

Reduces conflicting impulses that sabotage consistency and decision integrity.

Entry 11

Structural Code: **206530114**
Catalog ID: **CRP-02-06-0011**
Function: Protect (5)
Intensity: Class III
Variant: 011

Identity Integrity Lock

Deep protection against regression, people-pleasing overrides, and identity collapse.

Entry 12

Structural Code: **206620127**
Catalog ID: **CRP-02-06-0012**
Function: Amplify (6)
Intensity: Class II
Variant: 012

Self-Trust Amplifier

Amplifies self-trust signal so decisions become cleaner and less reactive.

Entry 13

Structural Code: **206410136**
Catalog ID: **CRP-02-06-0013**
Function: Repair (4)
Intensity: Class I
Variant: 013

Identity Fracture Repair

Repairs identity breaks after shame events, rejection, or prolonged inconsistency.

Entry 14

Structural Code: **206720145**
Catalog ID: **CRP-02-06-0014**
Function: Recalibrate (7)
Intensity: Class II
Variant: 014

Self-Definition Calibration

Aligns self-definition toward precision: fewer labels, stronger structure, cleaner boundaries.

Entry 15

Structural Code: **206110154**
Catalog ID: **CRP-02-06-0015**
Function: Stabilize (1)
Intensity: Class I
Variant: 015

Daily Identity Anchor

Reinforces identity stability as a daily baseline, even during emotional noise.

Entry 16

Structural Code: **206820163**
Catalog ID: **CRP-02-06-0016**
Function: Accelerate (8)
Intensity: Class II
Variant: 016

Commitment Execution Boost

Improves speed of execution once a decision is made (reduces hesitation delay).

Entry 17

Structural Code: **206220172**
Catalog ID: **CRP-02-06-0017**
Function: Increase (2)
Intensity: Class II
Variant: 017

Role Stability Capacity Increase

Increases capacity to hold stable roles (partner, leader, builder) without fragmentation.

Entry 18

Structural Code: **206320181**
Catalog ID: **CRP-02-06-0018**
Function: Decrease (3)
Intensity: Class II
Variant: 018

Regression Trigger Reduction

Reduces relapse triggers that pull identity back into old patterns under stress.

Entry 19

Structural Code: **206610196**
Catalog ID: **CRP-02-06-0019**
Function: Amplify (6)
Intensity: Class I
Variant: 019

Discipline Reinforcement (Identity)

Strengthens repeatable identity proof: routines, promises kept, consistent actions.

Entry 20

Structural Code: **206530205**
Catalog ID: **CRP-02-06-0020**
Function: Protect (5)
Intensity: Class III
Variant: 020

Sovereign Identity Anchor

Deep reinforcement of long-term identity stability under pressure and influence.

02-07 Attachment & Relationship Regulation

Domain 02 — Emotional & Identity

Focus:
- attachment security stabilization
- fear-of-abandonment loop reduction
- conflict reactivity control
- boundary stability under closeness
- clean communication under stress

Entry 1

Structural Code: **207120014**
Catalog ID: **CRP-02-07-0001**
Function: Stabilize (1)
Intensity: Class II
Variant: 001

Attachment Stability Anchor

Stabilizes attachment signal so closeness doesn't trigger volatility.

Entry 2

Structural Code: **207220027**
Catalog ID: **CRP-02-07-0002**
Function: Increase (2)

Intensity: Class II
Variant: 002

Secure Attachment Capacity Increase

Increases capacity for intimacy without threat-response activation.

Entry 3

Structural Code: **207310035**
Catalog ID: **CRP-02-07-0003**
Function: Decrease (3)
Intensity: Class I
Variant: 003

Abandonment Fear Reduction

Reduces abandonment anticipation and reassurance-seeking spikes.

Entry 4

Structural Code: **207420046**
Catalog ID: **CRP-02-07-0004**
Function: Repair (4)
Intensity: Class II
Variant: 004

Relationship Rupture Repair Reset

Supports recovery after conflict, withdrawal, or emotional rupture.

Entry 5

Structural Code: **207520053**
Catalog ID: **CRP-02-07-0005**
Function: Protect (5)
Intensity: Class II
Variant: 005

Boundary Containment Shield

Protects boundary stability during closeness, conflict, or pressure.

Entry 6

Structural Code: **207620069**
Catalog ID: **CRP-02-07-0006**
Function: Amplify (6)
Intensity: Class II
Variant: 006

Communication Clarity Amplifier

Strengthens clean, direct communication without emotional distortion.

Entry 7

Structural Code: **207710076**
Catalog ID: **CRP-02-07-0007**
Function: Recalibrate (7)
Intensity: Class I
Variant: 007

Attachment Signal Calibration

Recalibrates closeness signals away from threat and toward safety.

Entry 8

Structural Code: **207810088**
Catalog ID: **CRP-02-07-0008**
Function: Accelerate (8)
Intensity: Class I
Variant: 008

Conflict Downshift Acceleration

Improves speed of calming during disagreement or perceived rejection.

Entry 9

Structural Code: **207230094**
Catalog ID: **CRP-02-07-0009**
Function: Increase (2)
Intensity: Class III
Variant: 009

High-Security Bonding Surge

High-intensity increase of secure bonding signal and relational steadiness.

Entry 10

Structural Code: **207320103**
Catalog ID: **CRP-02-07-0010**
Function: Decrease (3)
Intensity: Class II
Variant: 010

Protest Behavior Reduction

Reduces chasing, testing, controlling, or escalating to regain closeness.

Entry 11

Structural Code: **207530114**
Catalog ID: **CRP-02-07-0011**
Function: Protect (5)
Intensity: Class III
Variant: 011

Attachment Integrity Lock

Deep protection against spiral cycles: withdrawal → panic → conflict.

Entry 12

Structural Code: **207620127**
Catalog ID: **CRP-02-07-0012**
Function: Amplify (6)
Intensity: Class II
Variant: 012

Trust Signal Amplifier

Strengthens trust baseline and reduces suspicion-driven interpretation.

Entry 13

Structural Code: **207410136**
Catalog ID: **CRP-02-07-0013**
Function: Repair (4)
Intensity: Class I
Variant: 013

Rejection Residue Repair

Repairs lingering sensitivity after perceived dismissal or emotional neglect.

Entry 14

Structural Code: **207720145**
Catalog ID: **CRP-02-07-0014**
Function: Recalibrate (7)
Intensity: Class II
Variant: 014

Reciprocity Calibration

Aligns giving/receiving dynamics toward balance (reduces overgiving and scoring).

Entry 15

Structural Code: **207110154**
Catalog ID: **CRP-02-07-0015**
Function: Stabilize (1)
Intensity: Class I
Variant: 015

Daily Connection Anchor

Reinforces a stable connection baseline without dependence or collapse.

Entry 16

Structural Code: **207820163**
Catalog ID: **CRP-02-07-0016**
Function: Accelerate (8)
Intensity: Class II
Variant: 016

Repair Speed Boost (Relational)

Improves speed of returning to calm connection after rupture.

Entry 17

Structural Code: **207220172**
Catalog ID: **CRP-02-07-0017**
Function: Increase (2)
Intensity: Class II
Variant: 017

Emotional Availability Increase

Increases capacity to stay present and responsive without shutdown.

Entry 18

Structural Code: **207320181**
Catalog ID: **CRP-02-07-0018**
Function: Decrease (3)
Intensity: Class II
Variant: 018

Jealousy Reactivity Reduction

Reduces threat spikes, comparison loops, and possessive escalation.

Entry 19

Structural Code: **207610196**
Catalog ID: **CRP-02-07-0019**
Function: Amplify (6)
Intensity: Class I
Variant: 019

Consistent Attachment Discipline Reinforcement

Strengthens steady behaviors that build secure attachment over time.

Entry 20

Structural Code: **207530205**
Catalog ID: **CRP-02-07-0020**
Function: Protect (5)
Intensity: Class III
Variant: 020

Secure Attachment Sovereignty Anchor

Deep reinforcement of long-term secure attachment and boundary stability.

02-08 Motivation System Repair

Domain 02 — Emotional & Identity

Focus:
• restoring drive after burnout
• reducing avoidance and freeze
• repairing reward circuitry "flatness"
• stabilizing follow-through
• rebuilding momentum without pressure spikes

Entry 1

Structural Code: **208120014**
Catalog ID: **CRP-02-08-0001**
Function: Stabilize (1)
Intensity: Class II
Variant: 001

Motivation Baseline Anchor

Stabilizes motivation as a usable daily baseline.

Entry 2

Structural Code: **208220027**
Catalog ID: **CRP-02-08-0002**
Function: Increase (2)
Intensity: Class II
Variant: 002

Drive Capacity Increase

Increases capacity to initiate action without overwhelm.

Entry 3

Structural Code: **208310035**
Catalog ID: **CRP-02-08-0003**
Function: Decrease (3)
Intensity: Class I
Variant: 003

Avoidance Reduction

Reduces avoidance behaviors and "I'll do it later" drift.

Entry 4

Structural Code: **208420046**
Catalog ID: **CRP-02-08-0004**
Function: Repair (4)
Intensity: Class II
Variant: 004

Burnout Recovery Reset

Repairs motivational fatigue and restores basic drive function.

Entry 5

Structural Code: **208520053**
Catalog ID: **CRP-02-08-0005**
Function: Protect (5)
Intensity: Class II
Variant: 005

Momentum Containment Shield

Protects momentum from collapse under stress or criticism.

Entry 6

Structural Code: **208620069**
Catalog ID: **CRP-02-08-0006**
Function: Amplify (6)
Intensity: Class II
Variant: 006

Reward Signal Amplifier

Strengthens the reward signal that makes effort feel worth it.

Entry 7

Structural Code: **208710076**
Catalog ID: **CRP-02-08-0007**
Function: Recalibrate (7)
Intensity: Class I
Variant: 007

Effort-to-Reward Calibration

Recalibrates expectations so progress feels real and trackable again.

Entry 8

Structural Code: **208810088**
Catalog ID: **CRP-02-08-0008**
Function: Accelerate (8)
Intensity: Class I
Variant: 008

Action Onset Acceleration

Improves speed of starting tasks once chosen.

Entry 9

Structural Code: **208230094**
Catalog ID: **CRP-02-08-0009**
Function: Increase (2)
Intensity: Class III
Variant: 009

High-Drive Surge

High-intensity reinforcement of drive and action capacity.

Entry 10

Structural Code: **208320103**
Catalog ID: **CRP-02-08-0010**
Function: Decrease (3)
Intensity: Class II
Variant: 010

Procrastination Reduction

Reduces delay loops, friction avoidance, and decision stalling.

Entry 11

Structural Code: **208530114**
Catalog ID: **CRP-02-08-0011**
Function: Protect (5)
Intensity: Class III
Variant: 011

Follow-Through Integrity Lock

Deep protection against quitting, drifting, or sabotaging momentum.

Entry 12

Structural Code: **208620127**
Catalog ID: **CRP-02-08-0012**
Function: Amplify (6)
Intensity: Class II
Variant: 012

Execution Clarity Amplifier

Strengthens clarity of next steps and reduces overwhelm noise.

Entry 13

Structural Code: **208410136**
Catalog ID: **CRP-02-08-0013**
Function: Repair (4)
Intensity: Class I
Variant: 013

Motivation Crash Repair

Repairs collapse after overwork, setbacks, or prolonged stagnation.

Entry 14

Structural Code: **208720145**
Catalog ID: **CRP-02-08-0014**
Function: Recalibrate (7)
Intensity: Class II
Variant: 014

Discipline Calibration

Aligns discipline toward steady output without intensity spikes.

Entry 15

Structural Code: **208110154**
Catalog ID: **CRP-02-08-0015**
Function: Stabilize (1)
Intensity: Class I
Variant: 015

Daily Drive Anchor

Reinforces stable daily drive, even on low-energy days.

Entry 16

Structural Code: **208820163**
Catalog ID: **CRP-02-08-0016**
Function: Accelerate (8)
Intensity: Class II
Variant: 016

Momentum Speed Boost

Improves speed of entering productive flow once started.

Entry 17

Structural Code: **208220172**
Catalog ID: **CRP-02-08-0017**
Function: Increase (2)
Intensity: Class II
Variant: 017

Persistence Capacity Increase

Increases capacity to persist without emotional collapse or avoidance.

Entry 18

Structural Code: **208320181**
Catalog ID: **CRP-02-08-0018**
Function: Decrease (3)
Intensity: Class II
Variant: 018

Freeze Response Reduction

Reduces shutdown/freeze patterns when tasks feel big or risky.

Entry 19

Structural Code: **208610196**
Catalog ID: **CRP-02-08-0019**
Function: Amplify (6)
Intensity: Class I
Variant: 019

Motivation Discipline Reinforcement

Strengthens consistent "show up" behavior over time.

Entry 20

Structural Code: **208530205**
Catalog ID: **CRP-02-08-0020**
Function: Protect (5)
Intensity: Class III
Variant: 020

Momentum Sovereignty Anchor

Deep reinforcement of long-term motivation stability and follow-through.

02-09 Consistency Under Pressure

Domain 02 — Emotional & Identity

Focus:
- execution under stress
- routine integrity during chaos
- volatility-to-discipline conversion
- relapse prevention after setbacks
- stable follow-through signal

Entry 1

Structural Code: **209120014**
Catalog ID: **CRP-02-09-0001**
Function: Stabilize (1)
Intensity: Class II
Variant: 001

Pressure-Proof Consistency Anchor

Stabilizes consistent action even when stress rises.

Entry 2

Structural Code: **209220027**
Catalog ID: **CRP-02-09-0002**

Function: Increase (2)
Intensity: Class II
Variant: 002

Discipline Capacity Increase

Increases capacity to stay on track under workload and emotional noise.

Entry 3

Structural Code: **209310035**
Catalog ID: **CRP-02-09-0003**
Function: Decrease (3)
Intensity: Class I
Variant: 003

Excuse-Loop Reduction

Reduces rationalization, avoidance logic, and "tomorrow" drift.

Entry 4

Structural Code: **209420046**
Catalog ID: **CRP-02-09-0004**
Function: Repair (4)
Intensity: Class II
Variant: 004

Routine Reset Protocol

Repairs consistency after disruption, travel, stress spikes, or missed days.

Entry 5

Structural Code: **209520053**
Catalog ID: **CRP-02-09-0005**
Function: Protect (5)
Intensity: Class II
Variant: 005

Routine Integrity Shield

Protects routines from sabotage, overwhelm, and emotional derailment.

Entry 6

Structural Code: **209620069**
Catalog ID: **CRP-02-09-0006**
Function: Amplify (6)
Intensity: Class II
Variant: 006

Follow-Through Signal Amplifier

Strengthens the internal "finish what you start" signal.

Entry 7

Structural Code: **209710076**
Catalog ID: **CRP-02-09-0007**
Function: Recalibrate (7)
Intensity: Class I
Variant: 007

Standard Maintenance Calibration

Recalibrates standards to sustainable output (no perfectionism collapse).

Entry 8

Structural Code: **209810088**
Catalog ID: **CRP-02-09-0008**
Function: Accelerate (8)
Intensity: Class I
Variant: 008

Task Re-Entry Acceleration

Accelerates return to action after interruption or hesitation.

Entry 9

Structural Code: **209230094**
Catalog ID: **CRP-02-09-0009**

Function: Increase (2)
Intensity: Class III
Variant: 009

High-Discipline Surge

High-intensity reinforcement of consistency under heavy pressure.

Entry 10

Structural Code: **209320103**
Catalog ID: **CRP-02-09-0010**
Function: Decrease (3)
Intensity: Class II
Variant: 010

Stress Derailment Reduction

Reduces the tendency to abandon routines when stress increases.

Entry 11

Structural Code: **209530114**
Catalog ID: **CRP-02-09-0011**
Function: Protect (5)
Intensity: Class III
Variant: 011

Consistency Lockout Shield

Deep protection against relapse into old patterns under pressure.

Entry 12

Structural Code: **209620127**
Catalog ID: **CRP-02-09-0012**
Function: Amplify (6)
Intensity: Class II
Variant: 012

Output Stability Amplifier

Amplifies stable daily output without burnout spikes.

Entry 13

Structural Code: **209410136**
Catalog ID: **CRP-02-09-0013**
Function: Repair (4)
Intensity: Class I
Variant: 013

Setback Residue Repair

Repairs the "I ruined it" mindset after misses, mistakes, or slip-ups.

Entry 14

Structural Code: **209720145**
Catalog ID: **CRP-02-09-0014**
Function: Recalibrate (7)
Intensity: Class II
Variant: 014

Pressure Response Calibration

Recalibrates stress response into controlled execution instead of shutdown.

Entry 15

Structural Code: **209110154**
Catalog ID: **CRP-02-09-0015**
Function: Stabilize (1)
Intensity: Class I
Variant: 015

Daily Discipline Anchor

Reinforces consistency as a daily baseline behavior.

Entry 16

Structural Code: **209820163**
Catalog ID: **CRP-02-09-0016**
Function: Accelerate (8)
Intensity: Class II
Variant: 016

Execution Speed Boost

Improves speed of action once a decision is made.

Entry 17

Structural Code: **209220172**
Catalog ID: **CRP-02-09-0017**
Function: Increase (2)
Intensity: Class II
Variant: 017

Persistence Capacity Increase

Increases ability to persist through boredom, resistance, and discomfort.

Entry 18

Structural Code: **209320181**
Catalog ID: **CRP-02-09-0018**
Function: Decrease (3)
Intensity: Class II
Variant: 018

Quit-Impulse Reduction

Reduces "scrap it" impulses when progress feels slow.

Entry 19

Structural Code: **209610196**
Catalog ID: **CRP-02-09-0019**
Function: Amplify (6)
Intensity: Class I
Variant: 019

Discipline Reinforcement (Behavioural)

Strengthens repeatable discipline habits through small consistent proofs.

Entry 20

Structural Code: **209530205**
Catalog ID: **CRP-02-09-0020**
Function: Protect (5)
Intensity: Class III
Variant: 020

Pressure Sovereignty Anchor

Deep reinforcement of long-term consistency under pressure and volatility.

02-10 Self-Sabotage Loop Reduction

Domain 02 — Emotional & Identity

Focus:
- interruption of self-defeat cycles
- reducing relapse after wins
- resistance + avoidance deactivation
- impulse containment under pressure
- clean follow-through protection

Entry 1

Structural Code: **210120014**
Catalog ID: **CRP-02-10-0001**
Function: Stabilize (1)
Intensity: Class II
Variant: 001

Self-Sabotage Stability Anchor

Stabilizes behavior to reduce sudden self-defeating decisions.

Entry 2

Structural Code: **210220027**
Catalog ID: **CRP-02-10-0002**
Function: Increase (2)

Intensity: Class II
Variant: 002

Forward-Motion Capacity Increase

Increases capacity to keep progressing without "undo" impulses.

Entry 3

Structural Code: **210310035**
Catalog ID: **CRP-02-10-0003**
Function: Decrease (3)
Intensity: Class I
Variant: 003

Self-Defeat Impulse Reduction

Reduces urges to quit, burn it down, or backtrack after progress.

Entry 4

Structural Code: **210420046**
Catalog ID: **CRP-02-10-0004**
Function: Repair (4)
Intensity: Class II
Variant: 004

Relapse Recovery Reset

Supports recovery after a sabotage event (binge, blow-up, abandonment of plan).

Entry 5

Structural Code: **210520053**
Catalog ID: **CRP-02-10-0005**
Function: Protect (5)
Intensity: Class II
Variant: 005

Momentum Protection Shield

Protects progress from emotional volatility and impulsive reversals.

Entry 6

Structural Code: **210620069**
Catalog ID: **CRP-02-10-0006**
Function: Amplify (6)
Intensity: Class II
Variant: 006

Integrity Signal Amplifier

Strengthens internal integrity: "do what you said you'd do."

Entry 7

Structural Code: **210710076**
Catalog ID: **CRP-02-10-0007**
Function: Recalibrate (7)
Intensity: Class I
Variant: 007

Reward-After-Win Calibration

Recalibrates the reflex to sabotage right after progress or success.

Entry 8

Structural Code: **210810088**
Catalog ID: **CRP-02-10-0008**
Function: Accelerate (8)
Intensity: Class I
Variant: 008

Loop Exit Acceleration

Accelerates the shift from impulse → control → correct action.

Entry 9

Structural Code: **210230094**
Catalog ID: **CRP-02-10-0009**
Function: Increase (2)
Intensity: Class III
Variant: 009

High-Integrity Surge

High-intensity reinforcement of self-control and long-horizon commitment.

Entry 10

Structural Code: **210320103**
Catalog ID: **CRP-02-10-0010**
Function: Decrease (3)
Intensity: Class II
Variant: 010

Resistance Behavior Reduction

Reduces avoidance, procrastination, and "I'll start over Monday" resets.

Entry 11

Structural Code: **210530114**
Catalog ID: **CRP-02-10-0011**
Function: Protect (5)
Intensity: Class III
Variant: 011

Sabotage Lockout Shield

Deep protection against repeated relapse cycling.

Entry 12

Structural Code: **210620127**
Catalog ID: **CRP-02-10-0012**
Function: Amplify (6)
Intensity: Class II
Variant: 012

Clean Choice Amplifier

Amplifies ability to choose the correct action under pressure.

Entry 13

Structural Code: **210410136**
Catalog ID: **CRP-02-10-0013**
Function: Repair (4)
Intensity: Class I
Variant: 013

Shame-Relapse Residue Repair

Repairs the "I messed up, so I may as well keep going" spiral.

Entry 14

Structural Code: **210720145**
Catalog ID: **CRP-02-10-0014**
Function: Recalibrate (7)

Intensity: Class II
Variant: 014

Identity-Action Alignment Calibration

Aligns behavior with chosen identity so actions stop contradicting goals.

Entry 15

Structural Code: **210110154**
Catalog ID: **CRP-02-10-0015**
Function: Stabilize (1)
Intensity: Class I
Variant: 015

Daily Integrity Anchor

Reinforces stable self-respect and consistent follow-through daily.

Entry 16

Structural Code: **210820163**
Catalog ID: **CRP-02-10-0016**
Function: Accelerate (8)
Intensity: Class II
Variant: 016

Re-Commit Speed Boost

Improves speed of returning to the plan after slips or hesitation.

Entry 17

Structural Code: **210220172**
Catalog ID: **CRP-02-10-0017**
Function: Increase (2)
Intensity: Class II
Variant: 017

Progress Tolerance Increase

Increases tolerance for progress without triggering fear, guilt, or self-punishment.

Entry 18

Structural Code: **210320181**
Catalog ID: **CRP-02-10-0018**
Function: Decrease (3)
Intensity: Class II
Variant: 018

Self-Punishment Reduction

Reduces destructive "payback" behaviors after mistakes or discomfort.

Entry 19

Structural Code: **210610196**
Catalog ID: **CRP-02-10-0019**
Function: Amplify (6)
Intensity: Class I
Variant: 019

Consistency Discipline Reinforcement

Strengthens small repeatable proofs that prevent relapse over time.

Entry 20

Structural Code: **210530205**
Catalog ID: **CRP-02-10-0020**
Function: Protect (5)
Intensity: Class III
Variant: 020

Long-Term Progress Sovereignty Anchor

Deep reinforcement of progress protection and sabotage resistance.

02-11 Internal Safety Installation

Domain 02 — Emotional & Identity

Focus:
• installing an internal safety baseline
• reducing "always on guard" signaling
• stabilizing body-mind permission to relax
• lowering internal threat interpretation
• restoring calm access under uncertainty

Entry 1

Structural Code: **211120014**
Catalog ID: **CRP-02-11-0001**
Function: Stabilize (1)
Intensity: Class II
Variant: 001

Internal Safety Baseline Anchor

Stabilizes the internal sense of safety as a default state.

Entry 2

Structural Code: **211220027**
Catalog ID: **CRP-02-11-0002**
Function: Increase (2)

Intensity: Class II
Variant: 002

Safety Capacity Increase

Increases capacity to feel safe without needing perfect conditions.

Entry 3

Structural Code: **211310035**
Catalog ID: **CRP-02-11-0003**
Function: Decrease (3)
Intensity: Class I
Variant: 003

Internal Threat Signal Reduction

Reduces background threat scanning and anticipatory tension.

Entry 4

Structural Code: **211420046**
Catalog ID: **CRP-02-11-0004**
Function: Repair (4)
Intensity: Class II
Variant: 004

Safety Restoration Reset

Repairs internal safety after stress events, conflict, or destabilizing days.

Entry 5

Structural Code: **211520053**
Catalog ID: **CRP-02-11-0005**
Function: Protect (5)
Intensity: Class II
Variant: 005

Safety Containment Shield

Protects calm baseline during uncertainty and external pressure.

Entry 6

Structural Code: **211620069**
Catalog ID: **CRP-02-11-0006**
Function: Amplify (6)
Intensity: Class II
Variant: 006

Safety Signal Amplifier

Amplifies the "it's safe now" signal in body and mind.

Entry 7

Structural Code: **211710076**
Catalog ID: **CRP-02-11-0007**
Function: Recalibrate (7)
Intensity: Class I
Variant: 007

Threat Appraisal Calibration (Safety)

Recalibrates interpretation away from danger-first assumptions.

Entry 8

Structural Code: **211810088**
Catalog ID: **CRP-02-11-0008**
Function: Accelerate (8)
Intensity: Class I
Variant: 008

Downshift Acceleration (Safety)

Improves speed of moving from guarded → regulated.

Entry 9

Structural Code: **211230094**
Catalog ID: **CRP-02-11-0009**
Function: Increase (2)
Intensity: Class III
Variant: 009

High-Safety Surge

High-intensity reinforcement of safety baseline installation.

Entry 10

Structural Code: **211320103**
Catalog ID: **CRP-02-11-0010**
Function: Decrease (3)
Intensity: Class II
Variant: 010

Hypervigilance Reduction

Reduces vigilance spikes, jumpiness, and alert-state persistence.

Entry 11

Structural Code: **211530114**
Catalog ID: **CRP-02-11-0011**
Function: Protect (5)
Intensity: Class III
Variant: 011

Safety Integrity Lock

Deep protection against abrupt destabilization and relapse into guard mode.

Entry 12

Structural Code: **211620127**
Catalog ID: **CRP-02-11-0012**
Function: Amplify (6)
Intensity: Class II
Variant: 012

Calm Access Amplifier

Amplifies access to calm without suppression or force.

Entry 13

Structural Code: **211410136**
Catalog ID: **CRP-02-11-0013**
Function: Repair (4)
Intensity: Class I
Variant: 013

After-Alarm Repair

Repairs lingering alarm residue after triggers or adrenaline events.

Entry 14

Structural Code: **211720145**
Catalog ID: **CRP-02-11-0014**
Function: Recalibrate (7)
Intensity: Class II
Variant: 014

Safety Set-Point Calibration

Aligns internal set-point toward safety as the assumed default.

Entry 15

Structural Code: **211110154**
Catalog ID: **CRP-02-11-0015**
Function: Stabilize (1)
Intensity: Class I
Variant: 015

Daily Safety Anchor

Reinforces a stable internal safety baseline each day.

Entry 16

Structural Code: **211820163**
Catalog ID: **CRP-02-11-0016**
Function: Accelerate (8)
Intensity: Class II
Variant: 016

Regulation Entry Speed Boost

Improves speed of entering regulated state when stress appears.

Entry 17

Structural Code: **211220172**
Catalog ID: **CRP-02-11-0017**
Function: Increase (2)
Intensity: Class II
Variant: 017

Safety Tolerance Increase

Increases tolerance for calm (reduces discomfort with stillness and quiet).

Entry 18

Structural Code: **211320181**
Catalog ID: **CRP-02-11-0018**
Function: Decrease (3)
Intensity: Class II
Variant: 018

Guard Mode Reduction

Reduces protective over-control behaviors and constant readiness stance.

Entry 19

Structural Code: **211610196**
Catalog ID: **CRP-02-11-0019**
Function: Amplify (6)

Intensity: Class I
Variant: 019

Safety Discipline Reinforcement

Strengthens repeatable safety maintenance behaviors and signals over time.

Entry 20

Structural Code: **211530205**
Catalog ID: **CRP-02-11-0020**
Function: Protect (5)
Intensity: Class III
Variant: 020

Internal Safety Sovereignty Anchor

Deep reinforcement of long-term internal safety stability under pressure.

2-12 Baseline Identity Reset

Domain 02 — Emotional & Identity

Focus:
• clearing stale self-definition
• interrupting legacy identity loops
• reset after rupture / burnout / change
• re-installing chosen identity baseline
• reducing "snapback" to old patterns

Entry 1

Structural Code: **212120014**
Catalog ID: **CRP-02-12-0001**
Function: Stabilize (1)
Intensity: Class II
Variant: 001

Identity Baseline Reset Anchor

Stabilizes the reset state so the system stops reverting to the old identity.

Entry 2

Structural Code: **212220027**
Catalog ID: **CRP-02-12-0002**
Function: Increase (2)
Intensity: Class II
Variant: 002

New Identity Capacity Increase

Increases capacity to hold a new self-definition without fracture.

Entry 3

Structural Code: **212310035**
Catalog ID: **CRP-02-12-0003**
Function: Decrease (3)
Intensity: Class I
Variant: 003

Old Self-Story Reduction

Reduces replay of legacy labels, narratives, and identity scripts.

Entry 4

Structural Code: **212420046**
Catalog ID: **CRP-02-12-0004**
Function: Repair (4)
Intensity: Class II
Variant: 004

Identity Damage Repair Reset

Repairs identity distortion after failure, humiliation, rejection, or prolonged instability.

Entry 5

Structural Code: **212520053**
Catalog ID: **CRP-02-12-0005**
Function: Protect (5)
Intensity: Class II
Variant: 005

Reset Integrity Shield

Protects reset progress from external influence and internal regression triggers.

Entry 6

Structural Code: **212620069**
Catalog ID: **CRP-02-12-0006**
Function: Amplify (6)
Intensity: Class II
Variant: 006

Chosen Identity Signal Amplifier

Amplifies the selected identity signal so actions align faster.

Entry 7

Structural Code: **212710076**
Catalog ID: **CRP-02-12-0007**

Function: Recalibrate (7)
Intensity: Class I
Variant: 007

Identity Reference Calibration

Recalibrates the internal "default self" reference toward the chosen baseline.

Entry 8

Structural Code: **212810088**
Catalog ID: **CRP-02-12-0008**
Function: Accelerate (8)
Intensity: Class I
Variant: 008

Identity Reset Acceleration

Accelerates disengagement from the old baseline and entry into the new.

Entry 9

Structural Code: **212230094**
Catalog ID: **CRP-02-12-0009**
Function: Increase (2)
Intensity: Class III
Variant: 009

High-Coherence Identity Surge

High-intensity reinforcement of identity coherence and role stability.

Entry 10

Structural Code: **212320103**
Catalog ID: **CRP-02-12-0010**
Function: Decrease (3)
Intensity: Class II
Variant: 010

Regression Pull Reduction

Reduces snapback pull toward the old identity under stress.

Entry 11

Structural Code: **212530114**
Catalog ID: **CRP-02-12-0011**
Function: Protect (5)
Intensity: Class III
Variant: 011

Baseline Lockout Shield (Old Identity)

Deep protection against relapse into legacy identity patterns.

Entry 12

Structural Code: **212620127**
Catalog ID: **CRP-02-12-0012**
Function: Amplify (6)
Intensity: Class II
Variant: 012

Self-Definition Clarity Amplifier

Amplifies clarity of identity language: who you are, what you do, what you tolerate.

Entry 13

Structural Code: **212410136**
Catalog ID: **CRP-02-12-0013**
Function: Repair (4)
Intensity: Class I
Variant: 013

Shame-Identity Fracture Repair

Repairs identity fragmentation caused by shame, regret, or self-contempt.

Entry 14

Structural Code: **212720145**
Catalog ID: **CRP-02-12-0014**
Function: Recalibrate (7)
Intensity: Class II
Variant: 014

Role Baseline Calibration

Calibrates identity around stable roles (builder, leader, provider, disciplined operator).

Entry 15

Structural Code: **212110154**
Catalog ID: **CRP-02-12-0015**
Function: Stabilize (1)
Intensity: Class I
Variant: 015

Daily Identity Reset Anchor

Reinforces the new baseline daily to prevent drift.

Entry 16

Structural Code: **212820163**
Catalog ID: **CRP-02-12-0016**
Function: Accelerate (8)
Intensity: Class II
Variant: 016

Implementation Speed Boost (Identity)

Improves speed of acting as the chosen identity without hesitation delay.

Entry 17

Structural Code: **212220172**
Catalog ID: **CRP-02-12-0017**
Function: Increase (2)
Intensity: Class II
Variant: 017

Identity Expansion Capacity Increase

Increases capacity to hold higher standards and higher responsibility without collapse.

Entry 18

Structural Code: **212320181**
Catalog ID: **CRP-02-12-0018**
Function: Decrease (3)
Intensity: Class II
Variant: 018

Self-Sabotage Identity Reduction

Reduces identity-linked sabotage (acting against goals to confirm old self-story).

Entry 19

Structural Code: **212610196**
Catalog ID: **CRP-02-12-0019**
Function: Amplify (6)
Intensity: Class I
Variant: 019

Identity Proof Reinforcement

Strengthens small repeatable proofs that stabilize identity through action.

Entry 20

Structural Code: **212530205**
Catalog ID: **CRP-02-12-0020**
Function: Protect (5)
Intensity: Class III
Variant: 020

Sovereign Baseline Anchor (Identity)

Deep reinforcement of long-term identity stability and resistance to regression.

02-13 Trigger Desensitization

Domain 02 — Emotional & Identity

Focus:
• trigger sensitivity reduction
• lowering "instant escalation" reflex
• separating present from past signal
• controlled exposure support (no flooding)
• faster return to baseline after activation

Entry 1

Structural Code: **213120014**
Catalog ID: **CRP-02-13-0001**
Function: Stabilize (1)
Intensity: Class II
Variant: 001

Trigger Stability Anchor

Stabilizes the system so triggers don't escalate as fast.

Entry 2

Structural Code: **213220027**
Catalog ID: **CRP-02-13-0002**
Function: Increase (2)
Intensity: Class II
Variant: 002

Exposure Tolerance Capacity Increase

Increases capacity to face mild triggers without overload.

Entry 3

Structural Code: **213310035**
Catalog ID: **CRP-02-13-0003**
Function: Decrease (3)
Intensity: Class I
Variant: 003

Trigger Sensitivity Reduction

Reduces sensitivity to known trigger cues (tone, words, environments).

Entry 4

Structural Code: **213420046**
Catalog ID: **CRP-02-13-0004**
Function: Repair (4)
Intensity: Class II
Variant: 004

Post-Trigger Reset

Repairs destabilization after a trigger event.

Entry 5

Structural Code: **213520053**
Catalog ID: **CRP-02-13-0005**
Function: Protect (5)
Intensity: Class II
Variant: 005

Trigger Containment Shield

Protects baseline during exposure windows and high-risk settings.

Entry 6

Structural Code: **213620069**
Catalog ID: **CRP-02-13-0006**
Function: Amplify (6)
Intensity: Class II
Variant: 006

Regulation Signal Amplifier (Trigger)

Strengthens regulation access while the trigger cue is present.

Entry 7

Structural Code: **213710076**
Catalog ID: **CRP-02-13-0007**
Function: Recalibrate (7)
Intensity: Class I
Variant: 007

Present-Signal Calibration

Recalibrates interpretation toward "present reality" over "past memory."

Entry 8

Structural Code: **213810088**
Catalog ID: **CRP-02-13-0008**
Function: Accelerate (8)
Intensity: Class I
Variant: 008

De-Escalation Acceleration

Improves speed of downshifting once activation starts.

Entry 9

Structural Code: **213230094**
Catalog ID: **CRP-02-13-0009**
Function: Increase (2)
Intensity: Class III
Variant: 009

High-Tolerance Surge (Exposure)

High-intensity increase of exposure tolerance without collapse response.

Entry 10

Structural Code: **213320103**
Catalog ID: **CRP-02-13-0010**
Function: Decrease (3)
Intensity: Class II
Variant: 010

Flash Reactivity Reduction

Reduces instantaneous emotional spike (snap/flare/panic start).

Entry 11

Structural Code: **213530114**
Catalog ID: **CRP-02-13-0011**
Function: Protect (5)
Intensity: Class III
Variant: 011

Trigger Loop Lockout Shield

Deep protection against repeated trigger cycling in a single day.

Entry 12

Structural Code: **213620127**
Catalog ID: **CRP-02-13-0012**
Function: Amplify (6)
Intensity: Class II
Variant: 012

Neutral Interpretation Amplifier

Amplifies neutral interpretation so cues stop defaulting to threat.

Entry 13

Structural Code: **213410136**
Catalog ID: **CRP-02-13-0013**
Function: Repair (4)
Intensity: Class I
Variant: 013

Trigger Residue Repair

Repairs lingering aftereffects: agitation, tension, rumination, shame.

Entry 14

Structural Code: **213720145**
Catalog ID: **CRP-02-13-0014**
Function: Recalibrate (7)
Intensity: Class II
Variant: 014

Cue-to-Meaning Calibration

Recalibrates the meaning assigned to cues (reduces overpersonalization).

Entry 15

Structural Code: **213110154**
Catalog ID: **CRP-02-13-0015**
Function: Stabilize (1)
Intensity: Class I
Variant: 015

Daily Desensitization Anchor

Reinforces gradual desensitization as a daily baseline process.

Entry 16

Structural Code: **213820163**
Catalog ID: **CRP-02-13-0016**
Function: Accelerate (8)
Intensity: Class II
Variant: 016

Recovery Speed Boost (Trigger)

Improves speed of returning to baseline after exposure.

Entry 17

Structural Code: **213220172**
Catalog ID: **CRP-02-13-0017**
Function: Increase (2)
Intensity: Class II
Variant: 017

Regulation Under Cue Increase

Increases capacity to stay regulated while the cue is present.

Entry 18

Structural Code: **213320181**
Catalog ID: **CRP-02-13-0018**
Function: Decrease (3)
Intensity: Class II
Variant: 018

Startle Response Reduction

Reduces startle/jolt reflex and rapid threat-body activation.

Entry 19

Structural Code: **213610196**
Catalog ID: **CRP-02-13-0019**
Function: Amplify (6)
Intensity: Class I
Variant: 019

Exposure Discipline Reinforcement

Strengthens consistent, controlled exposure behavior over time.

Entry 20

Structural Code: **213530205**
Catalog ID: **CRP-02-13-0020**
Function: Protect (5)
Intensity: Class III
Variant: 020

Trigger Sovereignty Anchor

Deep reinforcement of long-term trigger control and baseline stability.

02-14 Shame & Guilt Deactivation

Domain 02 — Emotional & Identity

Focus:
- shame loop interruption
- guilt overload reduction
- self-attack deactivation
- clean accountability without collapse
- restoring self-respect baseline

Entry 1

Structural Code: **214120014**
Catalog ID: **CRP-02-14-0001**
Function: Stabilize (1)
Intensity: Class II
Variant: 001

Shame Baseline Stabilization Anchor

Stabilizes shame levels so the system stops collapsing into self-contempt.

Entry 2

Structural Code: **214220027**
Catalog ID: **CRP-02-14-0002**
Function: Increase (2)
Intensity: Class II
Variant: 002

Self-Respect Capacity Increase

Increases capacity to hold self-respect even after mistakes.

Entry 3

Structural Code: **214310035**
Catalog ID: **CRP-02-14-0003**
Function: Decrease (3)
Intensity: Class I
Variant: 003

Self-Attack Reduction

Reduces internal punishment, self-insults, and harsh inner dialogue.

Entry 4

Structural Code: **214420046**
Catalog ID: **CRP-02-14-0004**
Function: Repair (4)
Intensity: Class II
Variant: 004

Shame Aftershock Repair Reset

Supports recovery after embarrassment, criticism, or exposure.

Entry 5

Structural Code: **214520053**
Catalog ID: **CRP-02-14-0005**
Function: Protect (5)
Intensity: Class II
Variant: 005

Emotional Dignity Shield

Protects stability so shame doesn't hijack behavior or decisions.

Entry 6

Structural Code: **214620069**
Catalog ID: **CRP-02-14-0006**
Function: Amplify (6)
Intensity: Class II
Variant: 006

Self-Compassion Signal Amplifier

Strengthens self-compassion without weakening accountability.

Entry 7

Structural Code: **214710076**
Catalog ID: **CRP-02-14-0007**
Function: Recalibrate (7)
Intensity: Class I
Variant: 007

Accountability Calibration

Recalibrates guilt into clean correction instead of collapse.

Entry 8

Structural Code: **214810088**
Catalog ID: **CRP-02-14-0008**
Function: Accelerate (8)
Intensity: Class I
Variant: 008

Shame Exit Acceleration

Improves speed of shifting out of shame states once they start.

Entry 9

Structural Code: **214230094**
Catalog ID: **CRP-02-14-0009**
Function: Increase (2)

Intensity: Class III
Variant: 009

High-Dignity Surge

High-intensity reinforcement of dignity, self-respect, and inner authority.

Entry 10

Structural Code: **214320103**
Catalog ID: **CRP-02-14-0010**
Function: Decrease (3)
Intensity: Class II
Variant: 010

Guilt Overload Reduction

Reduces excessive guilt and "I'm always wrong" bias.

Entry 11

Structural Code: **214530114**
Catalog ID: **CRP-02-14-0011**
Function: Protect (5)
Intensity: Class III
Variant: 011

Shame Lockout Shield

Deep protection against repeating shame spirals and self-erasure cycles.

Entry 12

Structural Code: **214620127**
Catalog ID: **CRP-02-14-0012**
Function: Amplify (6)
Intensity: Class II
Variant: 012

Neutral Self-View Amplifier

Amplifies a neutral self-view so events stop becoming identity verdicts.

Entry 13

Structural Code: **214410136**
Catalog ID: **CRP-02-14-0013**
Function: Repair (4)
Intensity: Class I
Variant: 013

Humiliation Residue Repair

Repairs lingering shame residue after social pain and rejection.

Entry 14

Structural Code: **214720145**
Catalog ID: **CRP-02-14-0014**
Function: Recalibrate (7)
Intensity: Class II
Variant: 014

Self-Value Calibration

Aligns self-value toward stable baseline (not performance-dependent).

Entry 15

Structural Code: **214110154**
Catalog ID: **CRP-02-14-0015**
Function: Stabilize (1)
Intensity: Class I
Variant: 015

Daily Self-Respect Anchor

Reinforces self-respect as a daily default state.

Entry 16

Structural Code: **214820163**
Catalog ID: **CRP-02-14-0016**
Function: Accelerate (8)
Intensity: Class II
Variant: 016

Recovery Speed Boost (Shame/Guilt)

Improves speed of returning to baseline after guilt/shame activation.

Entry 17

Structural Code: **214220172**
Catalog ID: **CRP-02-14-0017**
Function: Increase (2)
Intensity: Class II
Variant: 017

Repair-Action Capacity Increase

Increases capacity to take corrective action without self-hate.

Entry 18

Structural Code: **214320181**
Catalog ID: **CRP-02-14-0018**
Function: Decrease (3)
Intensity: Class II
Variant: 018

Worthlessness Signal Reduction

Reduces "I am bad / I don't deserve" identity-level shame signals.

Entry 19

Structural Code: **214610196**
Catalog ID: **CRP-02-14-0019**
Function: Amplify (6)
Intensity: Class I
Variant: 019

Dignity Discipline Reinforcement

Strengthens consistent dignity behaviors: boundaries, truth, and clean self-talk.

Entry 20

Structural Code: **214530205**
Catalog ID: **CRP-02-14-0020**
Function: Protect (5)
Intensity: Class III
Variant: 020

Shame Sovereignty Anchor

Deep reinforcement of long-term freedom from shame loops and identity collapse.

02-15 Emotional Resilience Expansion

Domain 02 — Emotional & Identity

Focus:
- expanding emotional capacity without hardening
- faster rebound after stress
- stability under uncertainty
- controlled intensity tolerance
- resilience as a baseline trait

Entry 1

Structural Code: **215120014**
Catalog ID: **CRP-02-15-0001**
Function: Stabilize (1)
Intensity: Class II
Variant: 001

Resilience Baseline Anchor

Stabilizes resilience as a daily baseline state.

Entry 2

Structural Code: **215220027**
Catalog ID: **CRP-02-15-0002**
Function: Increase (2)

Intensity: Class II
Variant: 002

Stress Capacity Increase

Increases capacity to carry stress without destabilizing.

Entry 3

Structural Code: **215310035**
Catalog ID: **CRP-02-15-0003**
Function: Decrease (3)
Intensity: Class I
Variant: 003

Collapse Reflex Reduction

Reduces collapse responses: shutdown, despair dips, and emotional quitting.

Entry 4

Structural Code: **215420046**
Catalog ID: **CRP-02-15-0004**
Function: Repair (4)
Intensity: Class II
Variant: 004

Resilience Recovery Reset

Supports recovery after high-pressure periods and setbacks.

Entry 5

Structural Code: **215520053**
Catalog ID: **CRP-02-15-0005**
Function: Protect (5)
Intensity: Class II
Variant: 005

Resilience Containment Shield

Protects baseline during prolonged stress and uncertainty.

Entry 6

Structural Code: **215620069**
Catalog ID: **CRP-02-15-0006**
Function: Amplify (6)
Intensity: Class II
Variant: 006

Emotional Endurance Amplifier

Strengthens endurance without numbing or suppression.

Entry 7

Structural Code: **215710076**
Catalog ID: **CRP-02-15-0007**
Function: Recalibrate (7)
Intensity: Class I
Variant: 007

Pressure Interpretation Calibration

Recalibrates stress interpretation away from threat and toward manageable load.

Entry 8

Structural Code: **215810088**
Catalog ID: **CRP-02-15-0008**
Function: Accelerate (8)
Intensity: Class I
Variant: 008

Rebound Acceleration

Improves speed of returning to baseline after disruption.

Entry 9

Structural Code: **215230094**
Catalog ID: **CRP-02-15-0009**
Function: Increase (2)

Intensity: Class III
Variant: 009

High-Resilience Surge

High-intensity reinforcement of resilience and stress tolerance capacity.

Entry 10

Structural Code: **215320103**
Catalog ID: **CRP-02-15-0010**
Function: Decrease (3)
Intensity: Class II
Variant: 010

Emotional Overload Reduction

Reduces overwhelm spikes and emotional flooding patterns.

Entry 11

Structural Code: **215530114**
Catalog ID: **CRP-02-15-0011**
Function: Protect (5)
Intensity: Class III
Variant: 011

Resilience Integrity Lock

Deep protection against collapse during extended stress windows.

Entry 12

Structural Code: **215620127**
Catalog ID: **CRP-02-15-0012**
Function: Amplify (6)
Intensity: Class II
Variant: 012

Calm Under Pressure Amplifier

Amplifies calm access during conflict, workload, and uncertainty.

Entry 13

Structural Code: **215410136**
Catalog ID: **CRP-02-15-0013**
Function: Repair (4)
Intensity: Class I
Variant: 013

Stress Residue Repair

Repairs lingering stress residue: agitation, fatigue, irritability.

Entry 14

Structural Code: **215720145**
Catalog ID: **CRP-02-15-0014**
Function: Recalibrate (7)
Intensity: Class II
Variant: 014

Emotional Range Expansion Calibration

Expands emotional range while keeping control and stability.

Entry 15

Structural Code: **215110154**
Catalog ID: **CRP-02-15-0015**
Function: Stabilize (1)
Intensity: Class I
Variant: 015

Daily Resilience Anchor

Reinforces resilience as a daily default trait.

Entry 16

Structural Code: **215820163**
Catalog ID: **CRP-02-15-0016**
Function: Accelerate (8)
Intensity: Class II
Variant: 016

Recovery Speed Boost (Resilience)

Improves speed of stabilizing after pressure spikes.

Entry 17

Structural Code: **215220172**
Catalog ID: **CRP-02-15-0017**
Function: Increase (2)
Intensity: Class II
Variant: 017

Uncertainty Tolerance Increase

Increases tolerance for uncertainty without anxiety escalation.

Entry 18

Structural Code: **215320181**
Catalog ID: **CRP-02-15-0018**
Function: Decrease (3)
Intensity: Class II
Variant: 018

Emotional Fragility Reduction

Reduces sensitivity that causes small stressors to create big crashes.

Entry 19

Structural Code: **215610196**
Catalog ID: **CRP-02-15-0019**
Function: Amplify (6)
Intensity: Class I
Variant: 019

Resilience Discipline Reinforcement

Strengthens daily resilience behaviors and long-term baseline stability.

Entry 20

Structural Code: **215530205**
Catalog ID: **CRP-02-15-0020**
Function: Protect (5)
Intensity: Class III
Variant: 020

Resilience Sovereignty Anchor

Deep reinforcement of long-term emotional resilience and stability under pressure.

PART II — INDEX ARCHITECTURE (VOLUME III)

Domain 02 — Emotional & Identity Calibration (300 Sequences)

DOMAIN INDEX

Domain 02 — Emotional & Identity Calibration
Subsystems: **02-01** → **02-15** (20 entries each)

SUBSYSTEM INDEX

02-01 Emotional Baseline Stabilization | CRP-02-01-0001–CRP-02-01-0020 | Codes 201110154–201820163
02-02 Anxiety Loop Reduction | CRP-02-02-0001–CRP-02-02-0020 | Codes 202110154–202820163
02-03 Trauma Load Containment | CRP-02-03-0001–CRP-02-03-0020 | Codes 203110154–203820163
02-04 Confidence & Authority Calibration | CRP-02-04-0001–CRP-02-04-0020 | Codes 204110154–204820163
02-05 Scarcity Imprint Deconstruction | CRP-02-05-0001–CRP-02-05-0020 | Codes 205110154–205820163
02-06 Identity Stability Reinforcement | CRP-02-06-0001–CRP-02-06-0020 | Codes 206110154–206820163
02-07 Attachment & Relationship Regulation | CRP-02-07-0001–CRP-02-07-0020 | Codes 207110154–207820163
02-08 Motivation System Repair | CRP-02-08-0001–CRP-02-08-0020 | Codes 208110154–208820163
02-09 Consistency Under Pressure | CRP-02-09-0001–CRP-02-09-0020 | Codes 209110154–209820163

02-10 Self-Sabotage Loop Reduction | CRP-02-10-0001–CRP-02-10-0020 | Codes 210110154–210820163

02-11 Internal Safety Installation | CRP-02-11-0001–CRP-02-11-0020 | Codes 211110154–211820163

02-12 Baseline Identity Reset | CRP-02-12-0001–CRP-02-12-0020 | Codes 212110154–212820163

02-13 Trigger Desensitization | CRP-02-13-0001–CRP-02-13-0020 | Codes 213110154–213820163

02-14 Shame & Guilt Deactivation | CRP-02-14-0001–CRP-02-14-0020 | Codes 214110154–214820163

02-15 Emotional Resilience Expansion | CRP-02-15-0001–CRP-02-15-0020 | Codes 215110154–215820163

ENTRY POSITION MAP (CONSISTENT ACROSS ALL SUBSYSTEMS)

Format: **2SS + Tail** (Tail = FI VVV + Check Digit)

E01 Stabilize (F1) Class II Tail **120014**
E02 Increase (F2) Class II Tail **220027**
E03 Decrease (F3) Class I Tail **310035**
E04 Repair (F4) Class II Tail **420046**
E05 Protect (F5) Class II Tail **520053**
E06 Amplify (F6) Class II Tail **620069**
E07 Recalibrate (F7) Class I Tail **710076**
E08 Accelerate (F8) Class I Tail **810088**
E09 Increase (F2) Class III Tail **230094**
E10 Decrease (F3) Class II Tail **320103**
E11 Protect (F5) Class III Tail **530114**
E12 Amplify (F6) Class II Tail **620127**
E13 Repair (F4) Class I Tail **410136**
E14 Recalibrate (F7) Class II Tail **720145**
E15 Stabilize (F1) Class I Tail **110154**
E16 Accelerate (F8) Class II Tail **820163**
E17 Increase (F2) Class II Tail **220172**
E18 Decrease (F3) Class II Tail **320181**

E19 Amplify (F6) Class I Tail **610196**
E20 Protect (F5) Class III Tail **530205**

FUNCTIONAL INDEX (FAST LOCATOR)

Stabilize (F1): **E01, E15**
Increase (F2): **E02, E09, E17**
Decrease (F3): **E03, E10, E18**
Repair (F4): **E04, E13**
Protect (F5): **E05, E11, E20**
Amplify (F6): **E06, E12, E19**
Recalibrate (F7): **E07, E14**
Accelerate (F8): **E08, E16**

INTENSITY INDEX (FAST LOCATOR)

Class I: **E03, E07, E08, E13, E15, E19**
Class II: **E01, E02, E04, E05, E06, E10, E12, E14, E16, E17, E18**
Class III: **E09, E11, E20**

THEMATIC KEYWORD INDEX (REFERENCE POINTERS)

Abandonment fear — CRP-02-07-0003, CRP-02-07-0010, CRP-02-07-0011
Accountability (clean) — CRP-02-14-0007, CRP-02-14-0017
Anxiety — CRP-02-02-0001, CRP-02-02-0010, CRP-02-02-0011
Avoidance — CRP-02-08-0003, CRP-02-08-0010, CRP-02-09-0003
Baseline (emotional) — CRP-02-01-0001, CRP-02-01-0015, CRP-

NUMERICAL CODE INDEX (ASCENDING)

202410136 — CRP-02-02-0013 202420046 — CRP-02-02-0004
202520053 — CRP-02-02-0005 202530114 — CRP-02-02-0011
202530205 — CRP-02-02-0020 202610196 — CRP-02-02-0019
202620069 — CRP-02-02-0006 202620127 — CRP-02-02-0012
202710076 — CRP-02-02-0007 202720145 — CRP-02-02-0014
202810088 — CRP-02-02-0008 202820163 — CRP-02-02-0016

203110154 — CRP-02-03-0015 203120014 — CRP-02-03-0001
203220027 — CRP-02-03-0002 203220172 — CRP-02-03-0017
203230094 — CRP-02-03-0009 203310035 — CRP-02-03-0003
203320103 — CRP-02-03-0010 203320181 — CRP-02-03-0018
203410136 — CRP-02-03-0013 203420046 — CRP-02-03-0004
203520053 — CRP-02-03-0005 203530114 — CRP-02-03-0011
203530205 — CRP-02-03-0020 203610196 — CRP-02-03-0019
203620069 — CRP-02-03-0006 203620127 — CRP-02-03-0012
203710076 — CRP-02-03-0007 203720145 — CRP-02-03-0014
203810088 — CRP-02-03-0008 203820163 — CRP-02-03-0016

204110154 — CRP-02-04-0015 204120014 — CRP-02-04-0001
204220027 — CRP-02-04-0002 204220172 — CRP-02-04-0017
204230094 — CRP-02-04-0009 204310035 — CRP-02-04-0003
204320103 — CRP-02-04-0010 204320181 — CRP-02-04-0018
204410136 — CRP-02-04-0013 204420046 — CRP-02-04-0004
204520053 — CRP-02-04-0005 204530114 — CRP-02-04-0011
204530205 — CRP-02-04-0020 204610196 — CRP-02-04-0019
204620069 — CRP-02-04-0006 204620127 — CRP-02-04-0012
204710076 — CRP-02-04-0007 204720145 — CRP-02-04-0014
204810088 — CRP-02-04-0008 204820163 — CRP-02-04-0016

205110154 — CRP-02-05-0015 205120014 — CRP-02-05-0001
205220027 — CRP-02-05-0002 205220172 — CRP-02-05-0017
205230094 — CRP-02-05-0009 205310035 — CRP-02-05-0003
205320103 — CRP-02-05-0010 205320181 — CRP-02-05-0018
205410136 — CRP-02-05-0013 205420046 — CRP-02-05-0004
205520053 — CRP-02-05-0005 205530114 — CRP-02-05-0011
205530205 — CRP-02-05-0020 205610196 — CRP-02-05-0019
205620069 — CRP-02-05-0006 205620127 — CRP-02-05-0012
205710076 — CRP-02-05-0007 205720145 — CRP-02-05-0014
205810088 — CRP-02-05-0008 205820163 — CRP-02-05-0016

206110154 — CRP-02-06-0015 206120014 — CRP-02-06-0001
206220027 — CRP-02-06-0002 206220172 — CRP-02-06-0017
206230094 — CRP-02-06-0009 206310035 — CRP-02-06-0003
206320103 — CRP-02-06-0010 206320181 — CRP-02-06-0018
206410136 — CRP-02-06-0013 206420046 — CRP-02-06-0004
206520053 — CRP-02-06-0005 206530114 — CRP-02-06-0011
206530205 — CRP-02-06-0020 206610196 — CRP-02-06-0019
206620069 — CRP-02-06-0006 206620127 — CRP-02-06-0012
206710076 — CRP-02-06-0007 206720145 — CRP-02-06-0014
206810088 — CRP-02-06-0008 206820163 — CRP-02-06-0016

207110154 — CRP-02-07-0015 207120014 — CRP-02-07-0001
207220027 — CRP-02-07-0002 207220172 — CRP-02-07-0017
207230094 — CRP-02-07-0009 207310035 — CRP-02-07-0003
207320103 — CRP-02-07-0010 207320181 — CRP-02-07-0018
207410136 — CRP-02-07-0013 207420046 — CRP-02-07-0004
207520053 — CRP-02-07-0005 207530114 — CRP-02-07-0011
207530205 — CRP-02-07-0020 207610196 — CRP-02-07-0019
207620069 — CRP-02-07-0006 207620127 — CRP-02-07-0012
207710076 — CRP-02-07-0007 207720145 — CRP-02-07-0014
207810088 — CRP-02-07-0008 207820163 — CRP-02-07-0016

208110154 — CRP-02-08-0015 208120014 — CRP-02-08-0001
208220027 — CRP-02-08-0002 208220172 — CRP-02-08-0017
208230094 — CRP-02-08-0009 208310035 — CRP-02-08-0003
208320103 — CRP-02-08-0010 208320181 — CRP-02-08-0018
208410136 — CRP-02-08-0013 208420046 — CRP-02-08-0004
208520053 — CRP-02-08-0005 208530114 — CRP-02-08-0011
208530205 — CRP-02-08-0020 208610196 — CRP-02-08-0019
208620069 — CRP-02-08-0006 208620127 — CRP-02-08-0012
208710076 — CRP-02-08-0007 208720145 — CRP-02-08-0014
208810088 — CRP-02-08-0008 208820163 — CRP-02-08-0016

209110154 — CRP-02-09-0015 209120014 — CRP-02-09-0001
209220027 — CRP-02-09-0002 209220172 — CRP-02-09-0017
209230094 — CRP-02-09-0009 209310035 — CRP-02-09-0003
209320103 — CRP-02-09-0010 209320181 — CRP-02-09-0018
209410136 — CRP-02-09-0013 209420046 — CRP-02-09-0004
209520053 — CRP-02-09-0005 209530114 — CRP-02-09-0011

209530205 — CRP-02-09-0020 209610196 — CRP-02-09-0019
209620069 — CRP-02-09-0006 209620127 — CRP-02-09-0012
209710076 — CRP-02-09-0007 209720145 — CRP-02-09-0014
209810088 — CRP-02-09-0008 209820163 — CRP-02-09-0016

210110154 — CRP-02-10-0015 210120014 — CRP-02-10-0001
210220027 — CRP-02-10-0002 210220172 — CRP-02-10-0017
210230094 — CRP-02-10-0009 210310035 — CRP-02-10-0003
210320103 — CRP-02-10-0010 210320181 — CRP-02-10-0018
210410136 — CRP-02-10-0013 210420046 — CRP-02-10-0004
210520053 — CRP-02-10-0005 210530114 — CRP-02-10-0011
210530205 — CRP-02-10-0020 210610196 — CRP-02-10-0019
210620069 — CRP-02-10-0006 210620127 — CRP-02-10-0012
210710076 — CRP-02-10-0007 210720145 — CRP-02-10-0014
210810088 — CRP-02-10-0008 210820163 — CRP-02-10-0016

211110154 — CRP-02-11-0015 211120014 — CRP-02-11-0001
211220027 — CRP-02-11-0002 211220172 — CRP-02-11-0017
211230094 — CRP-02-11-0009 211310035 — CRP-02-11-0003
211320103 — CRP-02-11-0010 211320181 — CRP-02-11-0018
211410136 — CRP-02-11-0013 211420046 — CRP-02-11-0004
211520053 — CRP-02-11-0005 211530114 — CRP-02-11-0011
211530205 — CRP-02-11-0020 211610196 — CRP-02-11-0019
211620069 — CRP-02-11-0006 211620127 — CRP-02-11-0012
211710076 — CRP-02-11-0007 211720145 — CRP-02-11-0014
211810088 — CRP-02-11-0008 211820163 — CRP-02-11-0016

212110154 — CRP-02-12-0015 212120014 — CRP-02-12-0001
212220027 — CRP-02-12-0002 212220172 — CRP-02-12-0017
212230094 — CRP-02-12-0009 212310035 — CRP-02-12-0003
212320103 — CRP-02-12-0010 212320181 — CRP-02-12-0018
212410136 — CRP-02-12-0013 212420046 — CRP-02-12-0004
212520053 — CRP-02-12-0005 212530114 — CRP-02-12-0011
212530205 — CRP-02-12-0020 212610196 — CRP-02-12-0019
212620069 — CRP-02-12-0006 212620127 — CRP-02-12-0012
212710076 — CRP-02-12-0007 212720145 — CRP-02-12-0014
212810088 — CRP-02-12-0008 212820163 — CRP-02-12-0016

213110154 — CRP-02-13-0015 213120014 — CRP-02-13-0001
213220027 — CRP-02-13-0002 213220172 — CRP-02-13-0017
213230094 — CRP-02-13-0009 213310035 — CRP-02-13-0003
213320103 — CRP-02-13-0010 213320181 — CRP-02-13-0018
213410136 — CRP-02-13-0013 213420046 — CRP-02-13-0004
213520053 — CRP-02-13-0005 213530114 — CRP-02-13-0011
213530205 — CRP-02-13-0020 213610196 — CRP-02-13-0019
213620069 — CRP-02-13-0006 213620127 — CRP-02-13-0012
213710076 — CRP-02-13-0007 213720145 — CRP-02-13-0014
213810088 — CRP-02-13-0008 213820163 — CRP-02-13-0016

214110154 — CRP-02-14-0015 214120014 — CRP-02-14-0001
214220027 — CRP-02-14-0002 214220172 — CRP-02-14-0017
214230094 — CRP-02-14-0009 214310035 — CRP-02-14-0003
214320103 — CRP-02-14-0010 214320181 — CRP-02-14-0018
214410136 — CRP-02-14-0013 214420046 — CRP-02-14-0004
214520053 — CRP-02-14-0005 214530114 — CRP-02-14-0011
214530205 — CRP-02-14-0020 214610196 — CRP-02-14-0019
214620069 — CRP-02-14-0006 214620127 — CRP-02-14-0012
214710076 — CRP-02-14-0007 214720145 — CRP-02-14-0014
214810088 — CRP-02-14-0008 214820163 — CRP-02-14-0016

215110154 — CRP-02-15-0015 215120014 — CRP-02-15-0001
215220027 — CRP-02-15-0002 215220172 — CRP-02-15-0017
215230094 — CRP-02-15-0009 215310035 — CRP-02-15-0003
215320103 — CRP-02-15-0010 215320181 — CRP-02-15-0018
215410136 — CRP-02-15-0013 215420046 — CRP-02-15-0004
215520053 — CRP-02-15-0005 215530114 — CRP-02-15-0011
215530205 — CRP-02-15-0020 215610196 — CRP-02-15-0019
215620069 — CRP-02-15-0006 215620127 — CRP-02-15-0012
215710076 — CRP-02-15-0007 215720145 — CRP-02-15-0014
215810088 — CRP-02-15-0008 215820163 — CRP-02-15-0016

STRUCTURAL DENSITY MAP

Per Subsystem (20 entries):
Stabilize **2** | Increase **3** | Decrease **3** | Repair **2** | Protect **3** | Amplify **3** | Recalibrate **2** | Accelerate **2**

Whole Volume (300 entries):
Stabilize **30** | Increase **45** | Decrease **45** | Repair **30** | Protect **45** | Amplify **45** | Recalibrate **30** | Accelerate **30**

Intensity Distribution:
Class I **90** | Class II **165** | Class III **45**

FINAL SYSTEM NOTE

Stability is not a mood.
It is a build.

Use this codex like an instrument: controlled, repeatable, measured.

APPENDICES

Appendix A — Code Generation Algorithm

A.1 Structural Code Format (9 digits)

D SS F I VVV C

- **D** = Domain (single digit)
  - o 1 = Financial Optimization
  - o 2 = Emotional & Identity

- $\circ$ 3 = Cognitive & Strategic
- $\circ$ 4 = Biological & Nervous System
- $\circ$ 5 = Advanced Structural Calibration
- **SS** = Subsystem (01–15)
- **F** = Function Type (1–8)
- **I** = Intensity Class (1–3)
- **VVV** = Variant / Entry Number (001–020)
- **C** = Option B Check-Digit (0–9)

Example: **213530114**
D=2, SS=13, F=5, I=3, VVV=011, C=4

A.2 Function Type Map

1. **Stabilize**
2. **Increase**
3. **Decrease**
4. **Repair**
5. **Protect**
6. **Amplify**
7. **Recalibrate**
8. **Accelerate**

A.3 Catalog ID Format

CRP-D-SS-EEEE

- D = 2-digit domain label (use "02" for Domain 2 in titles/TOC)
- SS = subsystem
- EEEE = entry sequence (0001–0020)

Example: **CRP-02-13-0011**

A.4 Generation Steps (per subsystem)

1. Set **D** (Domain digit) and **SS** (Subsystem).
2. For **VVV = 001–020**, assign **F** and **I** using the fixed Entry Position Map (Appendix C).
3. Generate **C** using Option B (Appendix B).
4. Concatenate: **DSSFI VVV C**.

Appendix B — Check-Digit Validation Logic (Option B)

B.1 Purpose

The check-digit exists to:

- prevent transcription errors
- enforce internal consistency
- make every code verifiable at a glance

B.2 Option B Check-Digit Table (VVV → C)

This system uses a **keyed 20-step validation cycle**.

001→4
002→7
003→5
004→6
005→3
006→9
007→6
008→8

009→4
010→3
011→4
012→7
013→6
014→5
015→4
016→3
017→2
018→1
019→6
020→5

B.3 Validation Procedure

Given a Structural Code **DSSFI VVV C**:

1. Extract **VVV** (positions 6–8 of the 9-digit code).
2. Look up expected check digit using the Option B table.
3. Compare to final digit **C**.
4. If mismatch → **invalid code**.

Strict validation (recommended): also confirm **F/I match the expected slot rules** for that VVV (Appendix C).

Appendix C — Sequential Allocation Rules

C.1 Fixed Subsystem Capacity

- Each subsystem contains **20 entries** (VVV 001–020).
- Each domain contains **15 subsystems** (SS 01–15).
- Total per domain: **300 sequences**.

C.2 Entry Position Map (Locks function + intensity by VVV)

This is the **master slot schedule** used in every subsystem.

VVV 001 → Stabilize (F1) Class II
VVV 002 → Increase (F2) Class II
VVV 003 → Decrease (F3) Class I
VVV 004 → Repair (F4) Class II
VVV 005 → Protect (F5) Class II
VVV 006 → Amplify (F6) Class II
VVV 007 → Recalibrate (F7) Class I
VVV 008 → Accelerate (F8) Class I
VVV 009 → Increase (F2) Class III
VVV 010 → Decrease (F3) Class II
VVV 011 → Protect (F5) Class III
VVV 012 → Amplify (F6) Class II
VVV 013 → Repair (F4) Class I
VVV 014 → Recalibrate (F7) Class II
VVV 015 → Stabilize (F1) Class I
VVV 016 → Accelerate (F8) Class II
VVV 017 → Increase (F2) Class II
VVV 018 → Decrease (F3) Class II
VVV 019 → Amplify (F6) Class I
VVV 020 → Protect (F5) Class III

C.3 Tail Construction Rule (FI VVV + C)

Tail = **F I VVV C**
Example (VVV 011): F=5, I=3, VVV=011, C=4 → **530114**

Appendix D — Intensity Distribution Matrix

D.1 Per Subsystem (20 entries)

- **Class I:** 6 entries
- **Class II:** 11 entries
- **Class III:** 3 entries

D.2 Per Domain (15 subsystems / 300 entries)

- **Class I:** 90
- **Class II:** 165
- **Class III:** 45

D.3 Functional Density (Per Domain / 300)

- Stabilize: 30
- Increase: 45
- Decrease: 45
- Repair: 30
- Protect: 45
- Amplify: 45
- Recalibrate: 30
- Accelerate: 30

Appendix E — Cross-Domain Stacking Guidelines

E.1 Rules (Non-Negotiable)

1. **One stack = one objective.** Don't mix objectives.
2. **Start with Stabilize.** If you skip stabilization, volatility rises.

3. **Only one Class III per stack.** Two Class III entries in one stack is not "stronger" — it's noisier.
4. **Stack duration is short.** Run stacks in defined windows, then reassess.

E.2 Standard Stack Types

Stack A — Baseline Control (3 codes)

- Stabilize (Class II)
- Decrease (Class I or II)
- Amplify (Class I or II)

Stack B — High-Pressure Lock (4 codes)

- Stabilize (Class II)
- Protect (Class II)
- Decrease (Class II)
- Accelerate (Class I)

Stack C — Fast Reset (2 codes)

- Repair (Class I or II)
- Accelerate (Class I)

Stack D — Expansion With Containment (5 codes)

- Stabilize (Class II)
- Increase (Class II)
- Amplify (Class II)
- Protect (Class II)
- Recalibrate (Class II)

E.3 Sequencing Rule

Stabilize → Reduce Noise → Increase Capacity → Protect → Accelerate

If you accelerate before stabilization, you amplify instability.

E.4 Safety Note (Clinical)

These sequences are **not medical or mental health treatment** and do not replace professional care. If symptoms are severe, escalating, or dangerous, use appropriate clinical support.

Appendix F — Scaling Framework to 2,500 Entries (Engineered Expansion)

F.1 Objective

Scale the system without diluting it.

The failure mode of most "code libraries" is uncontrolled expansion: more entries, less usability.

This framework prevents that.

F.2 Scaling Methods (Choose One Primary)

Method 1 — Add Subsystems (Cleanest)

- Keep 20-entry subsystems.
- Expand each domain from 15 → 25 subsystems.
- Result: 25 subsystems × 20 entries = **500 per domain**.

Method 2 — Add Micro-Sub-Variants (Controlled Density)

- Keep 15 subsystems.
- Add "micro-variants" inside each entry slot (A/B/C) only when needed.
- Result: 20 entries × 3 micro-variants = **60 per subsystem** (use sparingly).

Method 3 — Add Domains (Best Long-Term)

- Keep internal consistency.
- Introduce new domains only when they justify a full 300-entry map.

F.3 Anti-Dilution Rules

1. Every new subsystem must have a **unique operational purpose**.
2. Every entry must earn its place with a **distinct effect goal** (no synonyms).
3. Indices must update simultaneously:
   - subsystem index
   - functional index
   - intensity index
   - thematic keyword index
   - numerical code index

If it can't be indexed cleanly, it doesn't ship.

F.4 Scaling Target Example (2,500 Entries)

- 5 domains × 500 entries each = **2,500 total**
  Achieved by expanding each domain to **25 subsystems** (20 entries each).

BACK MATTER

FINAL SYSTEM NOTE

This volume is not "positive thinking."

It is structured correction.

If you use it like a ritual, you'll get random results.
If you use it like an instrument, you'll get repeatable outcomes.

Stability first.
Then expansion.
Then acceleration.

HOW TO NAVIGATE THE SERIES (FAST)

If your primary issue is money pressure:
→ **Volume I — Financial Optimization**

If your primary issue is sleep, fatigue, regulation, nervous system load:
→ **Volume II — Biological & Nervous System**

If your primary issue is anxiety, identity drift, shame, sabotage, emotional volatility:
→ **Volume III — Emotional & Identity Calibration**

If your primary issue is focus, strategy, decision-making, execution:
→ **Volume IV — Cognitive & Strategic Performance**

If you are stable and want advanced stacking + high-output calibration:
→ **Volume V — Advanced Structural Calibration**

OPERATING RULE (REMINDER)

If you are unstable, don't push intensity.

Use:

- Decrease (F3) + Stabilize (F1) + Protect (F5)
  Then reassess.

ABOUT THE AUTHOR

James Hutchinson builds structured reference systems.

The CRP Structural Codes™ series is designed to be:

- classified
- indexed
- tiered
- usable under real pressure

It is written to behave like a manual—not a belief system.

REVIEW REQUEST

If this book was genuinely usable for you, leave a short review.

One sentence is enough.
What did it help you stabilize, reduce, repair, or rebuild?

Your review is how this system survives in a marketplace full of noise.

www.ingramcontent.com/pod-product-compliance
Lightning Source LLC
Chambersburg PA
CBHW050916170626
46733CB00073B/1210